Maki

90 0914584 0

Gert J. J. Biesta

Editor

Making Sense of Education

Fifteen Contemporary Educational
Theorists in their own Words

 Springer

Editor
Gert J. J. Biesta
School of Education
University of Stirling
Stirling FK9 4LA
UK

ISBN 978-94-007-4016-7   ISBN 978-94-007-4017-4   (eBook)
DOI 10.1007/978-94-007-4017-4
Springer Dordrecht Heidelberg New York London

Library of Congress Control Number: 2012938866

Previously published in: Studies in Philosophy and Education, volume 30 issue 5, Fifty years of Studies in Philosophy and Education: A Special Anniversary Issue

Printed on acid-free paper

Springer is part of Springer Science+Business Media (www.springer.com)

*This book is dedicated to the memory of
Ilan Gur Ze'ev (1955–2012)*

Contents

Overview of Authors

Gert J. J. Biesta, University of Stirling, UK
Frank Margonis, University of Utah, USA
Clarence W. Joldersma, Calvin College, USA
Christiane Thompson, University of Halle, Germany
Tone Saevi, NLA Bergen, Norway
Lynn Fendler, University of Michigan, USA
Cris Mayo, University of Illinois USA
Ilan Gur-Ze'ev, University of Haifa, Israel
Carl Anders Säfström, Mälardalen University, Sweden
Barbara J. Thayer-Bacon, University of Tennessee, USA
Thomas Aastrup Rømer, Danish Pedagogical University, Denmark
Sharon Todd, University of Stockholm, Sweden
Charles Bingham, Simon Fraser University, Canada
Alexander M. Sidorkin, Rhodes College, USA
Jan Masschelein, University of Leuven, Belgium

About the Editor

Gert Biesta (www.gertbiesta.com) is Professor of Education at the School of Education, University of Stirling, and editor-in-chief of *Studies in Philosophy and Education*. In 2011–2012 he was President of the Philosophy of Education Society USA. He has published widely on the theory and philosophy of education and the theory and philosophy of social and educational research. Recent books include *Beyond Learning: Democratic Education for a Human Future (2006)*; *Good Education in an Age of Measurement: Ethics, Politics, Democracy* (2010); and *The Beautiful Risk of Education* (2012) (all with Paradigm Publishers); *Jacques Rancière: Education, Truth, Emancipation* (with Charles Bingham; Continuum Publishers 2010); *Derrida, Deconstruction, and the Politics of Pedagogy* (with Michael A. Peters; Peter Lang 2009); and *Learning Democracy in School and Society: Education, Lifelong Learning, and the Politics of Citizenship* (Sense Publishers 2011).

(Re)constructing the Theory and Philosophy of Education: An Introduction

Gert J. J. Biesta

This book provides an introduction into the theory and philosophy of education. It is not the first book that aims to introduce the field, and it will undoubtedly not be the last. How then is this book different? When we look at currently available introductions we can see that many, if not all of them, take a *systematic* approach, in that they aim to provide a structured overview of key concepts, ideas and themes, and of main traditions and schools of thought. This is sometimes done through a presentation of particular theorists and philosophers, but more often the focus is on themes and ideas, and the views of particular theorists and philosophers are discussed in function of such themes and ideas. Such introductions are necessarily *retrospective*. They look back at what has been achieved in the field so far, and do so from a certain distance, in order to be able to identify those ideas and positions that have proven to be important and influential. In this way such introductions provide newcomers with a clear map of what the field is about, a clear insight into how things hang together, and a clear indication of what the important and influential contributions are.

Yet such introductions not simply *represent* the field. By presenting a particular 'selection' of available work, and by presenting this in a particular way—showing particular connections; placing some work in the centre and other work in the margins—introductions to the field also contribute to the very *definition* of the field. We might say, therefore, that in addition to their *educative* function, introductions also perform a *political* function, in that they draw the boundaries of the field in a particular way. They thus contribute to the very construction of the field they aim to represent, or at least contribute to the consolidation of a particular construction of the field (see Toulmin 1972). The fact that most introductions to the field take a retrospective stance also means that they provide newcomers to the

G. J. J. Biesta (✉)
University of Stirling, Stirling FK9 4LA, UK
e-mail: gert.biesta@stir.ac.uk

G. J. J. Biesta (ed.), *Making Sense of Education*, DOI: 10.1007/978-94-007-4017-4_1,
© Springer Science+Business Media Dordrecht 2012

field with an overview of *end products* rather than with insights into the *processes* that have brought such end products about. In terms of Latour (1987, p.4), they provide newcomers with 'ready made science' rather than with 'science in the making.'

If this is what characterises most introductions to the theory and philosophy of education, then the present volume does indeed provide an entirely different 'entry' into the field. Its main distinctive quality is that it does not aim to provide a retrospective (re)construction of the field, but that it presents aspects of what is going on in the field right now, through fifteen original pieces of writing from contemporary educational theorists and philosophers in which they, in their own words, provide insights into their own thinking, their own concerns, and in their own forms of theory and theorising as it is currently unfolding. The pieces are therefore far less the 'polished' end products of their work and much more examples of thinking-in-action. They present theory and philosophy of education 'in the making'—to use Latour's phrase.

Doing so makes aspects of the theory and philosophy of education visible and accessible that tend to remain invisible in traditional introductions to the field. In this regard the present volume aims to be educative as well, but not by telling newcomers how the field should be understood, but by trying to open up what is going on in the field—right here and right now. The metaphor of the 'map' is therefore not really appropriate for what this book is about. The experience of engaging with this book is more like that of a tour of a building site; a site where things are still under construction and where buildings at different stages of completion can be found. While the approach taken in this book is therefore not very didactical—it is not a neat (re)presentation of what the theory and philosophy of education 'is' or is supposed to be—this precisely makes a different kind of engagement with the field possible. In this regard it also requires a different attitude from the reader; one in which the reader is less positioned as a learner—as someone who is supposed to learn about how the field is being represented by others—and more as a student—as one who is provided with material for study (see McClintock 1971; Biesta 2010a, b).

There is of course a risk involved in such an 'entry' to the field—which is why there are so many caution signs at building sites—as there is no guarantee that the particular selection presented in this book provides sufficient coverage of 'the field.' But that is precisely what this book aims to demonstrate as well, that is, that when we engage with theory and philosophy of education 'in the making' we do indeed not know its outcome; we do indeed not know how history will judge this work and will select between what is of enduring value or impact and what not. This makes this book no less political than many other introductions to the field, but it is perhaps a different kind of politics, not one that aims to police the field and draw and guard its boundaries, but rather one that aims to act as a reminder that the identity of a particular field is always the outcome of very particular processes, actions and interventions (see, again, Toulmin 1972; Latour 1987).

The contributions of this book have their origin in a special anniversary issue of the journal *Studies in Philosophy and Education*, which was published on the occasion of the fiftieth anniversary of the journal (see Biesta 2011a, b). While I could have chosen to look backwards by identifying the 'greatest hits' of the last 50 years, and while I could also have chosen to look forward by inviting authors to shed their light on the future of the field, I decided instead to look around me in order to see what might be going on in our field right now. That is why I invited contributions from scholars who, in a sense, I see as belonging to my generation. Doing so, as I explicitly acknowledged in the invitation letter, is fraught with difficulties, because what counts as a generation is very much a matter of perception from a particular position—in this case my position—and thus mainly reflects my own perceptions. Nonetheless I used this vague and in a sense arbitrary criterion to invite a number of scholars from a range of different countries to contribute a piece to this anniversary issue. As I didn't want to have total control over the selection of authors, I invited an initial group and asked them to provide me with further suggestions. The result is still a fairly arbitrary selection, but at least it is not a selection that was entirely made by me.

Rather than asking for reflections on the field, I invited the contributors to write a short piece outlining their own theory, philosophy, account or understanding of education. I asked the contributors not only to be as explicit as possible, but also encouraged them to be explicitly self-referential, that is, taking their own body of work as the main frame of reference. I invited them, in other words, to speak and also to speak as much as possible in their own voice—which is the reason why I asked for single-authored contributions. With this I was also responding to a tendency in at least some countries that authors—particularly doctoral students—by default have to list their supervisors as co-authors on all their work. While I do strongly believe in the value of academic generosity, such practices do raise important questions about voice, authorship and authorly responsibility. The reason why I asked for accounts of the authors' theories or philosophies of education—which means that I asked them to start from educational issues rather than philo-sophical ones—partly has to do with my own academic history. I was educated in a tradition that does not see philosophy of education as a branch of applied philosophy firmly rooted, intellectually and institutionally, in philosophy (for a representation of such a view see, for example, Curren 2003), but rather conceives of it as a form of educational scholarship that makes use of philosophical resources but which has its intellectual 'home' in the field of education. This tradition, which is strongly influenced by the way in which the field of education has developed in the German speaking world, puts educational questions and interests first and sees philosophy as one of the potential resources to enrich reflection on these issues. While there are clear points of connection between this more Continental approach and what in the English language is called 'philosophy of education'—and it is important to bear in mind that this phrase cannot be simply and straightforwardly translated into other languages—it does provide a slightly different angle on the interconnections and encounters between philosophy and education (see also Biesta 2011c).

As *Studies in Philosophy and Education* sees itself as an international journal, I have always found it important to maintain an awareness of the different ways in which the encounter between education and philosophy has taken shape in different contexts and traditions (see also Biesta 2010b). This is why I did *not* ask the contributors for a piece on 'my favourite philosopher,' 'my favourite philosophy,' or 'my favourite theory,' but rather invited them to *do* theory and philosophy of education from the range of traditions in which their work is rooted. The contributions to this book—which are reprinted from the special issue—thus provide a fascinating collection of points of view, some clearly situated in the traditions of philosophy of education that have come to fruition in the English-speaking world; others clearly located in what we might call Continental approaches. The contributions that follow not only represent a wide and interesting range of ideas and perspectives and a wide and interesting range of educational and political commitments. They also present an interesting range of different forms and styles of writing and articulation, thus also making visible in the *form* of writing that this is work 'in the making' rather than a finished and polished end product that simply follows the conventions of academic publishing.

References

Biesta, G.J.J. (2010a). Learner, student, speaker. Why it matters how we call those we teach. *Educational Philosophy and Theory, 42*(4), 540–552.

Biesta, G.J.J. (2010b). Editorial: Publishing in studies in philosophy and education. *Studies in Philosophy and Education, 29*(1), 1–4.

Biesta, G.J.J. (ed) (2011a). Fifty years of Studies in Philosophy and Education: A Special Anniversary Issue. *Studies in Philosophy and Education, 30*(5).

Biesta, G.J.J. (2011b). An adventure in publishing revisited. Fifty years of Studies in Philosophy and Education. *Studies in Philosophy and Education, 30*(5), 429–432.

Biesta, G.J.J. (2011c). Disciplines and theory in the academic study of education: A Comparative Analysis of the Anglo-American and Continental Construction of the field. *Pedagogy, Culture and Society, 19*(2), 175–192.

Curren, R. (Ed) (2003). *A companion to the philosophy of education.* Oxford: Wiley-Blackwell.

Latour, B. (1987). *Science in action. How to follow scientists and engineers through society.* Milton Keynes: Open University Press.

McClintock, R. (1971). Toward a place for study in a world of instruction. *Teachers College Record, 73*(2), 161–205.

Toulmin, S. (1972). *Human understanding: The collective use and evolution of concepts.* Oxford: Clarendon Press.

In Pursuit of Respectful Teaching and Intellectually-Dynamic Social Fields

Frank Margonis

Published online: 20 April 2011
© Springer Science+Business Media B.V. 2011

Abstract In contrast to educational policies in the U.S., which assume an individualistic path of success and promote the assimilation of students, this essay argues for pedagogies where teachers focus upon facilitating the development of strong relationships en route to creating exciting educational environments and fertile contexts for social justice movements. Powerful teachers model the process whereby a commitment to appreciating the perspectives of individual students is combined with the orchestration of a dynamic intersubjective context, because such contexts call out the strongest performances of individuals. Viewing educational events in terms of the patterns and rhythms that transpire in a particular social fields allows educators ways to create powerful educational environments even in neocolonial contexts that pit students and teachers against one another. Viewing educational events as social fields also allows us to understand how the common classroom, which focuses each student on the material in front of them, creates impotent individuals who dissociate themselves from others.

Keywords Relational educational philosophy · Student-centered pedagogy · Neocolonial educational contexts

As an educational philosopher situated in the United States, I have sought to develop a counter-hegemonic collectivist pedagogical orientation devoted to creating exciting educational environments and fertile contexts for social justice movements. Seeking healthy collectivities in the U.S. is complicated by the nation's cut-throat economy combined with its colonial history–both of which pit individuals and groups against one another. A pervasive culture of competition renders individuals isolated and impotent, and the nation's colonial history has left us with deep relational wounds, separating people who have endured forms of colonial attack–such as American Indians, African Americans, and Latinas/os–from European descendant peoples. The fault lines of class and race predict

F. Margonis (✉)
Department of Education, Culture and Society, 1705 E. Campus Center Drive,
Rm. 307, Salt Lake City, UT 84112-9256, USA
e-mail: frank.margonis@utah.edu

success and failure in U.S. schools, and to justify the large-scale exclusion of working-class and previously-colonized peoples from access to good jobs and political influence, the nation has forged a callous domestic ethic.[1] A narrative asserting that every individual who wishes to succeed, can do so (if only they work hard enough), transfers the responsibility for educational failures to the excluded students. Presuming that individuals have control over their own destinies, and are responsible for their own behavior, educators dismiss students who do not approximate some white middle-class norm–practices I find to be both miseducative and unjust.

This dismissal of "other people's children" signals the need for an educational language and practice which embodies a far more appreciative understanding of students and a far more generous search for the conditions that will enable all students to thrive. We need an educational praxis that will enact what Martin Luther King called a "radical revolution in values," from a "thing-oriented society to a person-oriented society"(King 2001, 157–8). To pursue Dr. King's call in education, we will need a way of affirming students and teachers, despite the austere bureaucratic contexts of schooling and despite the tragic chasms created by economic competitiveness and colonial legacies. My hope is that relational philosophies of education can contribute to the creation of a person-oriented ethos in education by offering more nuanced and appreciative portraits of students and teachers and by offering teachers and students new conceptual tools for facilitating exciting educational events and powerful collectivities.

We see educational expressions of a thing-oriented society when "national interests," economic competitiveness, and the education of "human capital" are prioritized, neglecting the legacies of racial and economic segregation which create huge polarities between the preparatory educations offered many privileged students and what Laurence Parker and myself called education for the "containment" of inner-city African American and Latina/o students (Margonis and Parker 1995; Margonis 1989). We see the expressions of a thing-oriented society when students, who are denied healthy educational relationships in U.S. schools, are objectified using deficit descriptors–such as, "culturally deprived" or "at risk"–which mark them as undeserving people (Margonis 1992). With macroscopic currents in the U.S. accentuating the nation's inequalities, I have turned my philosophical attention to localized moments of possibility, that is, toward developing pedagogical orientations that might aid educators in creating meaningful educational events which counter the impact of societal hierarchies.

Pursing a "person-oriented" educational ethic involves, first and foremost, an appreciation of the importance of showing students respect–something one finds in the works of Jean-Jacques Rousseau. One of the most disturbing traits of educational policy in the contemporary U.S. is the implied lack of respect granted to the ways of thinking, talking, and acting students bring to schools. National educational policy has been designed to assimilate students to a national identity–an aim many students and parents have resented; for previously-colonized groups, assimilation is an especially-offensive goal, because it calls upon students to believe in the superiority of a nation that continues to relegate them to a subordinate place in society. Philosophically, assimilationist designs are made possible by conceptions of human nature which portray people as highly malleable–such as, John Locke's *tabula rasa*–and bestow value on people more in terms of who they may become

---

[1] School success and failure is rarely discussed in relation to the colonial history of the U.S., even though the late John Ogbu offered a convincing corpus of research which showed that the greatest educational inequalities in the U.S. were experienced by people he called "involuntary minorities," that is, people who were brought into the nation by force. See Ogbu (1974).

and less in terms of who students are right now (Margonis 1998). In contrast, Rousseau offered an educational vision in which "the child's nature"–not the designs of political leaders or the desires of teachers–would serve as the premier ethical guide. Rousseau suggested that children have patterns of growth and a relation to their environment that, thanks to providential design, operate to the child's benefit and will continue to operate regardless of whether educators and parents know and heed these natural dictates. Rousseau's Emile seeks to describe these natural patterns of learning and growth so informed educators might be able to follow the path marked out by nature (Rousseau 1979).

Believing that it is a teacher's role to discern patterns at play in educational events which are already in operation, and adapt educational interventions to those patterns, I have suggested a relational rewriting of Rousseau's position:

> Instead of asking after the child's nature and its place in the providential order, the teacher—from this perspective—should ask, "What can the students and myself be, given who we are?" While such a question cannot lead to the full articulation of a teacher's educational aims, it might allow her to develop aims that are organic outgrowths of her educational relationships and prevent her from creating aims which ignore the students' ways of being in the world.(Margonis 1999, 249)

By adapting to the patterns of interaction that occur between students and teachers, educators betray an "ontological attitude." Even though I do not have Rousseau's faith that following the path of nature is a matter of following God's design, I do believe that the relational patterns that occur amongst students and teachers have a power which must be respected if educational events are to be respectful and educationally exciting.

Contemporary educational philosophers, Todd (2003) and Biesta (2006), have articulated theories inspired by Emmanuel Levinas, which strengthen and complement Rousseau's account of respecting students. Rousseau tells us to follow the path of nature–which I interpret to mean the relational give-and-take which emerges in a relationship–but he never problematizes educators' knowledge of that path. Todd and Biesta argue that educators can never know the other, that whenever teachers act upon their "knowledge" of the other, they pursue their own desires and not the needs of students. Educators are obliged to "listen to the alterity of the other" and respond to her utterances. If we combine Rousseau's pedagogical humility with Todd's and Biesta's exhortations to listen to the alterity of the other, we can envision educators who seek both to understand and adapt to the intersubjective patterns that transpire with their students, while recognizing that their "knowledge" of these patterns are no more than informed guesses, which are always secondary to the students' own statements, which call teachers to respond.

The development of respectful relationships is a prerequisite to powerful educational events, and one finds visionary portraits of educational exchanges in the student-centered tradition. Dewey's (1980) portrait of cooperative inquiry organized by the scientific method, and Freire's (1993) description of egalitarian, de-colonizing dialogue–are both offered as a means of setting in motion social spaces of focused, passionate intellectual intensity, which call upon students and teachers to extend their abilities. Both men conceive of education as a social event–not as a matter of passing down knowledge. Both men emphasize the process whereby students and teachers come to know, which forces us to consider the complex and multifarious ways in which people think and act. Both men deemphasize the teacher's authority, and neither values a student's ability to repeat their teacher's words, but instead asks for intersubjective engagement and the construction of situation-specific knowledge. Both discourage summary judgements concerning a student's ability and instead focus upon the social conditions that call out admirable student performances. Both men took fundamental steps away from the patterns of surveillance and control that have characterized the teacher-centered pedagogies they sought to displace. Despite these powerful steps, it seems to me that Dewey's and Freire's respective visions remain constrained by their reliance upon humanistic language.

Indeed, it may be Dewey's humanism which undergirds exclusionary aspects of student-centered pedagogies. Delpit (1995) has argued that student-centered pedagogies often exclude students who are not from the "culture of power," perhaps because–given the operations of cultural difference and power in U.S. classrooms–only some students act like the ideal student imagined in the pedagogies. Dewey envisions groups of students who use the scientific method to think their way through problems, and the steps of scientific thought–such as posing hypotheses and observing consequences–are said to be rooted in the biological tendencies of humans to struggle for survival. I've tried to show that in Dewey's writings, Dewey's universalistic portrait of the problem solver is implicitly white and middle-class; the schools Dewey envisioned were largely populated by European-descendant students and the forms of cooperation Dewey envisioned were forged in these homogeneous contexts. The communication patterns of white-Black racial polarization, described by W.E.B. Du Bois in his school experiences, do not enter into Dewey's conception of the problem-solving classroom. Had African American youth entered one of Dewey's early 20th Century classrooms, the onus may well have fallen upon them to figure out the rules of the cooperative problem-solving game and to claim a place in the game despite the exclusionary acts of white youth (Margonis 2009). The humanistic language in Freire's pedagogy appears in his central ideal–the education of critically-conscious activists–and in his characterization of "oppressed" students. The essentialized characterization of oppressed students in Freire's writing unfortunately operates in a way that is akin to other deficit descriptors, to characterize students in wholesale fashion without coming to terms with their specific abilities. And the ideal of a critically-conscious activist, like Dewey's cooperative problem solver, offers an at once enobling, and limiting, vision (Margonis 2000).

As Biesta (2006) suggests, humanistic ideals limit the pluralism of pedagogies and lead to educational acts of exclusion and assimilation; thus, the ideal of critical consciousness leads educators to respond favorably only to students who dialogue in the way expected of a critically-conscious activist, while teachers attempt to bring wayward students around to the ideal (Margonis forthcoming). A relational pedagogical language allows us to de-couple Dewey's and Freire's visionary pedagogies from the humanistic language that limits their pluralism. We would do well to embrace cooperative forms of inquiry for which Dewey argued, as one way of organizing pedagogical spaces, recognizing that there are many ways for students to work cooperatively and that one method of thinking should probably not be specified in advance. Similarly, Freire's relational portrait of educational dialogue is especially exciting if we focus on Freire's insistence upon trusting, nonhierarchical student–teacher relationships and a free flow of discussion devoted to understanding the economic and political contradictions in the students' lives. Instead of expecting one form of dialogue, however, educators, would do well to invite broad and cacophonous forms of interaction into the classroom; a mix of conservative, artistic, comedic, and narrative patterns in the classroom gives a broader range of points of contact with students and clues them that a particular educational space offers many avenues of entry.

By focusing upon the character of meaningful educational relationships, and not upon the specific human traits students are said to possess or upon the traits a pedagogy is designed to produce, relational philosophies of education have the potential to offer more

nuanced and humane interpretations of educational events, while expanding the pedagogical possibilities for powerful educational interactions. For instance, when the students
in Eliot Wigginton's high school English classroom expressed their dissatisfaction by
burning his podium, he showed a relational perspective in asking himself–not, "who is to
blame for this?"–but, "what am I doing to call out such determined resistance?" Wigginton showed a relational orientation when he responded to the students by confessing his
limitations as a teacher and asking students for their help in carrying out the class. He
further showed a relational orientation when he pursued extended discussion and planning
with the students which led to reconceiving the social space of the classroom: the curriculum, the patterns of discussion and decision making, the products students would
produce–because all these factors come together to shape the educational dynamic that
develops (Margonis 2004).

To theorize the sophistication embodied in Wigginton's actions, we might turn to
Gadamer (1975), who directs our attention to the rhythms and patterns of a social field.
Instead of assuming individuals who are in control of their actions, Gadamer says the game
plays the players. If we view educational events in an analogous way, we might say that the
patterns and rhythms of educational interactions lead to, or close off, student expressions,
and that the character of classroom interactions shapes the types of expressions made
possible. Yet, unlike games, social fields may have rules from a variety of contexts being
enacted alongside one another; students are played by the rules from their own intersubjective contexts, in juxtaposition to the other students and the teacher, who are played by
the rules of their intersubjective contexts. As students and teachers engage in communicative give-and-take, various performances come to be accepted, and new rules emerge
which come to be constitutive of a particular educational space. Participants develop a
sense of which ways of speaking and acting are indeed welcome in this space (and which
statements or acts may not be welcome)–which is sometimes referred to as the "climate"
or "atmosphere" of that space. When students and teachers talk about educational events,
they cite many factors which shape their sense of what can or cannot be said: the political
and social character of the communities surrounding the educational space, the respective
histories students and teachers bring to the space, the policies of the school and messages
those policies send regarding the trust placed in players, the practices and demeanor of the
teacher, the mix of students in the class, the curriculum to which they are called upon to
respond–to name some of the most salient factors. Powerful teachers seek to orchestrate the
development of a social space that includes all the students and allows them to express
themselves in educationally-valuable ways.

Viewing educational spaces as social fields with rhythms and patterns of communication allows us to assess the dynamism of the educational relationships in play, for the
quality of the relationships shapes the richness of possible educational exchanges. There
are times, such as when the students set fire to Wigginton's podium, that fruitful patterns of
communication are simply closed off; in this case, the teacher's didacticism met with
student disinterest and resentment. When Wigginton confessed his inability to carry out the
class without the students' help, he changed the signals–addressing the students respect-
fully, as collaborators–and successfully opened channels of communication. When he set
before the class the task of designing an English curriculum that would excite the students
and enable them to learn substantive writing skills, he–in a Deweyan project-oriented way–
set in motion an unbounded set of discussions that led to highly engaged, intellectual
investigation. This task orientation allowed Wigginton's class to develop rich and layered,
academically rich, discussions, culminating in the production of the *Foxfire* magazine.
The relationships students built with Wigginton allowed them to achieve high scholarly

standards; students had set themselves a remarkably demanding task, and they pursued the critical discussions and negotiations that would allow them to accomplish their aims collectively (Margonis 2004).

In contrast to Wigginton's classroom, many students and teachers within U.S. schools remain caught within intersubjective games which play out the painful and oppressive legacies of class and race polarization. Even highly-committed educators inadvertently find themselves becoming police officers when faced with resistant students, who are defined as deficient by the discourses of the larger society (Margonis 2007). Assimilationist and individualistic worldviews offer only the worst form of guidance in these contexts: resistant students are blamed, documented, expelled. Transforming adversarial intersubjective exchanges into dynamic social fields of interest and inquiry is profoundly difficult, yet we have examples of teachers who accomplish this very task. The teachers described by Ladson-Billings (1994) and the Highlander Folk School teachers, Septima Clark and Myles Horton (Payne 1995)–model pedagogical orientations which create dynamic social fields with subaltern students in neocolonial contexts. Such teachers find ways of evading the police officer-inmate dynamic by making superogatory pedagogical gestures which signal to students the teacher's distaste for the surveillance students face in their daily lives and the teacher's dedication to respecting and responding to each of the students. Such teachers attend carefully to the intersubjective dynamics that transpire amongst the students and themselves and develop means of steering the intersubjective field towards interaction patterns that will draw students out; when students speak, the teacher listens carefully to whatever they say, including that which is beyond comprehension. Such teachers find ways to create mutually-supportive intersubjective social fields, believing that students can only find their own voices when they are in a social context which facilitates their efforts of expression. To help create the conditions for such a space to emerge, teachers adapt the curriculum to fit the students' interests, their ways of thinking, and their political orientations. They also tend to the quality of relationships within the classroom space as a whole–connecting students to one another and insisting that each student feels response(able) to attend to and think with their peers (Margonis 2011). The teachers of Highlander went further to embody a unique form of asymmetrical solidarity: they committed themselves–both pedagogically and politically–to the independent understandings each student developed in dialogue with other students and the teacher, without expecting any reciprocal show of solidarity on the student's part (Margonis 2008).

Teachers such as those described by Ladson-Billings illustrate the power of viewing educational events as a social field, for it is here that we can witness the multiple strategies used to transform a polarized social context into a supportive and dynamic one. The power the game has over the players is also visible in the orderly classroom, where each student is expected to devote themselves, individually, to the curriculum in the name of passing a test. In such a miseducative space, students are effectively cut off from the intersubjective connections that would be most educative and are instead, prepared to live in social fields of isolation and impotence. And it is these sorts of social fields that may well lead people to disassociate themselves from "other people's children."

Acknowledgment   The Author wishes to thank Gert Biesta for the invitation to summarize his educational philosophy. The Author's efforts to respond to his invitation surely overstates the degree of consistency and clarity of the project–coming as it is, 20 years into an uncertain process of feeling his way, often clumsily. The author also wishes to thank Donna Deyhle for her helpful comments on this manuscript.

References

Biesta, G. (2006). *Beyond learning*. Boulder, CO: Paradigm Publishers.

Delpit, L. (1995). *Other people's children*. New York: New Press.

Dewey, J. (1980). Democracy and education. In J. Boydston (Ed.), *The middle works* (pp. 1899–1924). Carbondale: Southern Illinois University Press.

Freire, P. (1993). *Pedagogy of the oppressed*. M. Ramos, trans. New York: Continuum.

Gadamer, H.-G. (1975). *Truth and method*. New York: Continuum.

King, M. L. (2001). Beyond vietnam. In C. Carson & K. Shepard (Eds.), *A call to conscience*. New York: Grand Central Publishing.

Ladson-Billings, G. (1994). *The dreamkeepers*. San Francisco: Jassey-Bass Publishers.

Margonis, F. (1989). What is the meaning of contemporary educational nationalism? In J. Giarelli (Ed.), *Philosophy of education: 1988* (pp. 343–352). Normal: Philosophy of Education Society.

Margonis, F. (1992). The cooptation of at risk: Paradoxes of policy criticism. *Teachers College Record, 94*, 343–364.

Margonis, F. (1998). Dewey and the arrogance of reason. In S. Laird (Ed.), *Philosophy of education: 1997* (pp. 365–373). Urbana: Philosophy of Education Society.

Margonis, F. (1999). The demise of authenticity. In S. Tozer (Ed.), *Philosophy of education: 1998* (pp. 248–257). Urbana: Philosophy of Education Society.

Margonis, F. (2000). Relational pedagogy without foundations. In R. Curren (Ed.), *Philosophy of education: 1999* (pp. 99–107). Urbana: Philosophy of Education Society.

Margonis, F. (2004). From student resistance to educative engagement. In A. Sidorkin & C. Bingham (Eds.), *No education without relation* (pp. 39–54). Mahwah: Lawrence Erlbaum.

Margonis, F. (2007). Seeking openings of already closed student-teacher relationships. In D. Vokey (Ed.), *Philosophy of education: 2006* (pp. 176–184). Urbana: Philosophy of Education Society.

Margonis, F. (2008). A relational ethic of solidarity? In B. Stengel (Ed.), *Philosophy of education: 2007*. Urbana: Philosophy of Education Society.

Margonis, F. (2009). John Dewey's racialized visions of the student and classroom community. *Educational Theory, 59*, 17–39.

Margonis, F. (2011). Tending neocolonial gaps. In G. Biesta (Ed.), *Philosophy of education: 2010*. Urbana: Philosophy of Education Society.

Margonis, F. (forthcoming). Addressing students responsively and critically. In R. Kunzman (ed.), *Philosophy of education: 2011*. Urbana: Philosophy of Education Society.

Margonis, F., & Parker, L. (1995). Choice, privatization, and unspoken strategies of containment. *Educational Policy, 9*, 375–403.

Ogbu, J. (1974). *The next generation*. New York: Academic Press.

Payne, C. (1995). *I've got the light of freedom*. Berkeley: University of California Press.

Rousseau, J-J. (1979). *Emile*. A. Bloom, trans. New York: Basic Books.

Todd, S. (2003). *Learning from the other*. Albany: State University of New York.

Education: Understanding, Ethics, and the Call of Justice

Clarence W. Joldersma

Published online: 9 April 2011
© Springer Science+Business Media B.V. 2011

Abstract   Education is interpreted as something basic to our humanity. As part of our primordial way of being human, education is intrinsic to the understanding's functioning. At the same time education involves an originary ethical relation to the other, unsettling the self-directed character of the striving to live. And because of its social setting, the call of many others, education orients one to the social, to the call of justice.

Keywords   Understanding · Ethics · Call of justice · Improvisational handiness · Distantiation · Interpretation · Affordances · World · Earth · Conatus · Primordial way of being human · The other · Inspiration · Enjoyment · Anxiety

Many discussions of education, including my own, involve critiques of formal schooling (Deakin Crick and Joldersma 2007; Joldersma and Deakin Crick 2010). However, in the very possibility of such criticism lays the idea that education is not the same as schooling, instead forming an implicit frame from which such critique can be launched. In my own case I have often argued that schooling needs to heed more clearly the call of ethics and justice (Joldersma 2002, 2006, 2008a, b, 2009a). This critique suggests that something more basic frames schooling, something that we might call education.

In this essay I will focus directly on education as such. I will sketch out a more fundamental understanding of education, depicting it as something intrinsic to the very fabric of being human. I will first connect the notion of education to a primordial way of being human, something I will call *understanding*. I will join this to the idea that an originary relation with others calls one's understanding to account, something I will call *ethics*. Connecting education to understanding, a primordial way of being human, in the context of an originary ethical relation, brings to view its basic character. These two will jointly create the possibility of interpreting education as something fundamental.

To interpret education in this manner requires a brief foray into primordial ways of being as humans. As I have developed more fully elsewhere, humans are living creatures

C. W. Joldersma (✉)
Education Department, Calvin College, 3201 Burton S.E, Grand Rapids, MI 49546, USA
e-mail: cjolders@calvin.edu

constituted from anonymous earthly elements (Joldersma 2008a). It is as if the fabric of the earth folded back onto itself, forming localized points of bounded interiority. Biologically and existentially, humans are complex systems of stable organization in dynamic relation with an external milieu. The system's boundary makes room for a certain level of freedom from its exterior. But the continued achievement of such interiorized freedom itself relies on life's heightened complexity, including a dependent, dynamic relation with its surroundings. This means that the independence of freedom paradoxically necessitates continual renewal and structural vigil against the inexorable forces of its surroundings to which it would otherwise yield. As such, human embodiment is novel independence that is at the same time heightened vulnerability, a duality of bodily intentionality. This preconscious intentionality can be thought of as *conatus*, the striving to live.

Striving to live occurs on earth. As such, conatus shows itself in two distinct, albeit related, modes. On the one hand, it involves a primal freedom that manifests itself most basically as enjoyment (Joldersma 2008a). Primordial freedom involves enjoying one's connection to the earth, marking the freedom of an independent interiority that finds itself in an environment through the joy of incoming sensibility. On the other hand, conatus involves a dependency that shows itself as anxiety. Primordial dependence involves being anxious about life's inescapable exposure and vulnerability to earth's potentially threatening forces (Joldersma 2009b). Precisely because the freedom of independence is conditioned by openness, the generosity of support of an enjoyable earth simultaneously is felt as the threat of a rumbling contingency to that life by that very same earth. The conatus associated with human embodied life is based simultaneously in a qualitatively novel enjoyable independence and in an emergent heightened anxious dependence. Enjoyment and worry are modes of being situated on earth (see also Joldersma 2009c).

The modes of striving to live on earth color the way we find ourselves living in a world. A world is a web of meanings within which humans are embedded and which are formed and reformed by our interactions with our environment. The meanings associated with living in a world show themselves most basically as possible affordances for engagement with our surroundings. Affordances are manifest prototypically through our handiness— exploring, touching, seeing, grasping, moving in, and manipulating our surroundings (see also Joldersma 2005). Through such handiness, which includes all our bodily engagements, the surroundings disclose themselves as possibilities to satisfy our strivings for life, enhancing the security of enjoyable living and dampening the threat to life of earth's vagaries. Meaning is most deeply the possible relations and practices associated with our safekeeping of earth's generosity, enhancing our enjoyment in security, while keeping at bay its threatening contingency, diminishing our anxiousness in vulnerability.

Perhaps because humans are a generalist species, living in a variety of bioregions in which we did not originate and for which we are not necessarily natively well suited, we cope in a less than determined way. By coping I mean enacted handiness aimed at enhancing life's security and reduces its danger. Perhaps precisely because humans are generalists, we are on the one hand able to *exploit* the amazing variety of habitats while on the other are not *instinctively* able cope well for life and flourishing. Although the success of coping is grounded in biologically-structured sensorimotor interactions with the milieu, it is something non-instinctive and improvisational. This generalized, contingent handiness supplements the lack of hard-wired nature. Because handiness is improvisational and non-instinctive in character, its generalized anticipations constitute what can be called *understanding*.

Understanding has an anticipatory character, something that situates humans in a meaningful world. Understanding's disclosures are provisional and possible, revealing the world's *possible* affordances and our *possible* actions of improvisational handiness. Precisely because of its anticipatory character, understanding does not supply ready-made ways of engaging one's surroundings. Or conversely, because handiness is not instinctual, it is constituted through the possible ways our surroundings are available for use and interaction. Colored by the modes of anxiety and enjoyment, the possibilities of the understanding are embodied in the improvisationality of handiness, affording possible new meanings, anticipating possible new uses of things, interpreting the ways that the world shows itself for novel roles, actions and constructions. Understanding's anticipatory character is a forwarding projection of contingent possibilities for ever more successful ways of underdetermined coping. Understanding is, in this interpretation, a primordial way humans are in the world (see also Joldersma 2009c).

The understanding's anticipatory possibilities are not mere bare engagements with the world; instead, human handiness is oriented towards the creation of *dwellings*. Dwellings are successful mediating structures that protect against earth's rumbling contingency while harnessing the resources of earth's generosity. The modes of anxiety and enjoyment orient the understanding's disclosure of possibilities towards the meanings associated with dwelling. At its most basic, the possibilities of availability—including material, place, use, relation, purpose—are meaningful in connection to ways of dwelling. Actual dwellings are the result of enacted handiness that have committed to the affordances disclosed in understanding. Although we rightly think of homes and other immediate shelters as dwellings, they extend to the dizzying array of possible and actual social structures, interaction patterns, institutions, organizations, regulations and practices. The creation of successful dwellings is not based in something instinctive, however, but as enacted improvisational handiness. As such, constructing dwellings forms the goal of handiness, a way of being intentionally within the world. Understanding is the embodied intentionality that anticipates the world *as* something so that dwellings can be successful in their mediation. Understanding is central in our primordial way inhabiting a world and living on earth via dwellings.

The mode of conatus we identified as vulnerability reveals also an original openness to other humans. Relationships with others take us into the realm of the ethical. By *ethics* I mean to indicate an asymmetric relation where the other human, as *other*, has a rightful claim on oneself. More strongly, the ethical breaks through the *self-directed* preservational character of conatus by calling one to responsibility. The core of the ethical relationship involves being responsible to another human, precisely as other rather than as a being like oneself. This shows itself in the understanding. The particulars of one's improvisational handiness, the understanding's projective possibilities, are not present ready-made, full-blown, let alone as if emerging entirely from within. Instead, from the day we are born, the increasing success of one's enacted handiness arises in openness to others, from interactions with their own improvisational prompts. Fundamental to understanding is human interdependence—a reliance on others for developing increased discriminations of our surroundings, improving the possibilities of improvisational handiness in creating successful dwellings. The very character of human understanding discloses the permanent possibility for, and inescapability of, human interdependence. The ethical thus manifests itself with respect to the understanding in a relation to the other that falls outside of one's anticipatory possibilities. As an ethical relation, the other is precisely outside of the reach of one's provisional interpretations of the world, while legitimately breaking through the particularities of those interpretations by calling them to account.

Of course, there is never just a single other with whom one has an ethical relationship. There is a third, a fourth, and a fifth. The ethical relation to any one other human is always in the context of others, third parties we could call them (see Joldersma 2009a). This takes understanding beyond the individual ethical relation, into the realm of justice. Justice is a question of treating *each* other responsibly in the context of *all* the others. Justice requires comparison between others, even though each is unique and incomparable. The requirement of justice thus gives rise to conscious deliberation, reflective consciousness, a thoughtfulness that distances oneself from the immediate, singular responsibility. Justice is the collective call of *each* other on oneself, and by thoughtful extension, on each other human. The call of justice is the composite pull of all the ethical claims that each other makes on all the others, situating the ethical relation into a social matrix, the responsibility one has to *each* other in the context of *all* the others. Earlier I noted that social structures are ways of dwelling together, sedimented results of improvisational handiness that have remained over time in the quest to enhance a refuge for enjoyment and to diminish the hazards of life's vagaries. But dwellings can also rightly be interpreted as responses to the network of ethical claims of each other on all the others, that dwellings are also always situated within the call of justice.

Implicit throughout this entire discussion is education. Education is the contingent, non-instinctual, formative, dynamic development of understanding that occurs as we live with others in order to dwell together justly. We can identify education with both the understanding's non-instinctual anticipations of meaning for successful dwelling and its need *for* and responsibility *to* the other in the context of others to dwell with justice.

The improvisational, anticipatory character of the understanding reveals its educational necessity. Understanding's non-instinctual quality means that its continued development depends fundamentally on contingently acquired new anticipatory meanings. Its anticipatory nature, as possibilities, reveals understanding as something general, where the particulars of its projective possibilities require non-determined, i.e., educational, development. This includes the need to refine one's improvisational handiness and to add to one's repertoire of sensorimotor intentionalities. The modes of enjoyment and anxiety that orient understanding are not enough, but require education for successful mediating structures and practices that shelter. To live successfully on earth requires being educated about how to create dwellings. Successful living requires that one's understanding is developed in such a way that one's agency in creating stability and security of dwelling can be successful. Understanding fundamentally involves education. Because of understanding's nature, education is itself a central feature of the primordial condition of being human.

The primordial character of education is revealed in the understanding's inability not to be influenced by something incoming. The standing possibility of being disturbed discloses the understanding as a space for possible new meanings, new uses of things, and new ways of interpreting the world. The troubling character of such disturbances is their intrusion into the complacencies and settledness of one's interpretations of the world, including the adequacies of one's action in the world. One's enjoyment of settledness can always be disturbed by something coming from the outside. The freedom associated with the understanding's independence can always be called to account from a site outside of one's anticipations. More strongly, the possibility of being questioned is a core feature of one's understanding—current interpretations and possible actions are always vulnerable to being upset. Education names this permanent inability to refuse disturbance. Education's primordial character is thus situated in the possibility of being disturbed, involving something incoming that disquiets before one has the ability to judge its propriety. Education is grounded in an inescapable exposure to something that comes in from the outside, a disturbance I have called inspiration (Joldersma 2008a). Inspiration breaks up the naiveté of one's understanding, showing its impermanence and contingency.

Inspiration uncovers education's mode of action. Disturbances in one's understanding does not by itself lead to more successful enacted handiness. Rather, inspiration shows possible inadequacies through a process of *distantiation*. More adequate interpretations of the world require a distancing from one's current provisional, partial, and possible understandings, something that happens by having one's own interpretations and actions called to account from the outside. This creates the space for arousing a critical posture towards oneself with respect to one's anticipations. Being called up short creates a gap between the projective possibilities of the understanding and one's naïve enjoyment of current anticipations. It is the process of distancing that makes disruptions into educative possibilities. Education occurs when an outside influence pulls one away from one's own current understandings. Being disrupted creates a space for questioning oneself. Distantiation is what makes possible being a question to oneself. Inspiration marks an originary, educative interdependence.

Inspiration, the disturbance that distances oneself from one's self-satisfaction and naïve enjoyment, typically comes from a relation to another *human being*. It is the other's calling one to account that creates the distance exposing the finitude and partiality of one's understanding. The relation to the other puts education into the realm of the ethical. The ethical inspiration that constitutes education involves the other, as a teacher. The other, as teacher, is located outside of one's understanding (Joldersma 2002, 2008a). The teacher has a rightful claim in calling one's anticipations to account. The core of this educational relation involves being responsible to the other precisely as teacher. Being responsible is disclosed through the distantiation that undermines one's felt self-sufficiency. The rupture of one's enjoyable understanding is directed, in being answerable to another human. More strongly, the distancing relation arising from the other *decenters* the self-centeredness of one's understanding in the struggle to live. Education is thus situated, fundamentally, in a relationship to another human being, as other. Education involves an asymmetric relation to someone who is outside of one's understanding. That is, the other is not just one of the projective possibilities within the anticipatory structure of understanding. Instead, the other who calls one's understanding to account, is located outside of one's expectations and anticipations, i.e., outside of one's world. It is precisely from that distance that one's understanding can be called into question. Education can thus be construed as something for which one is structurally never quite ready. Being ready means being able to assimilate the incoming into one's current interpretations of the world, without significant change. It means being able to anticipate what is incoming. But that is the opposite of educationally being disturbed by something, being called into question. Education is always a little belated, precisely because it is a response to a teacher's questioning, unexpected and unforeseen. Education occurs, it seems, only when one arrives a little late to the teacher's disturbing intrusion.

Of course, for education to be ethical, the teacher's claim must not be felt as violent; instead, it must be welcomed (Joldersma 2011). Welcome returns us to the metaphor of dwelling, here expanded as the place from where one is hospitable to something incoming. Dwelling is a home, the comfortable place of familiarity from which one welcomes, a porous boundary where something or someone on the outside is invited in. The possibility of welcome shows oneself to already be dwelling somewhere, a particular place of meaningful familiarity. Without the familiarity that epitomizes one's dwelling, there could be no welcoming the disturbance of other as teacher, no educational hospitality for strangeness. That is, one must already, through the anticipatory structure of the understanding, be living in a meaningful world, a world interpreted in particular ways through enacted improvisational handiness. Without an anchor in such freedom and independence, there would be no education, for then one could not welcome the distancing force of its disturbance. This invitation is also what makes the disturbance ethical, and as such, educational. The possibility of education means that one goes willingly against the grain of one's own freedom in understanding. As such, education is always hopeful. Hope is the expectation of something new and better beyond what one can anticipate. Thus the welcome associated with education is welcoming the unforeseen, something that comes from beyond the anticipatory projections of one's understanding. Hope is expecting something which one cannot foresee, an embodied response to inspiration. The ethical that helps constitute education involves such hope, through welcoming the disturbance that comes from the other as teacher.

Because of its relational character, education occurs in a social context. One's ethical responsibility to the other as teacher is compounded and divided by the existences of others as possible teachers. *Each* other human can be an other, someone located outside of one's understanding, who might call one's interpretations up short. With respect to one's understanding, there are other others who also stand outside of one's anticipations. This fundamental plurality rightfully divides one's attention and responsibility, showing the need for thoughfulness. One's thoughtfulness requires further distantiation, away from the particular call embedded in each educational relationship, giving rise to a more fully-orbed reflective consciousness that deliberates about how to limit responsibility to any particular other in order to do justice to the other others. Education in its social matrix involves the responses one makes to the composite pull of all the claims made by many others as teachers. The educational response to any one other as teacher is thus social in character, situated in justice. The need to weigh and deliberate one's being questioned shows education's social character to be connected to the call of justice.

But the call of justice intrinsic to education goes further. The ethical disturbances of education also invite one to reorient one's interpretations and actions outwardly, for the sake of others, towards the welfare of third parties. The possibility of justice in the collective success of human dwelling depends on goodness, an inversion of one's striving for oneself, a reorienting of oneself towards the flourishing of others. The call of justice shows up when the others' claims on oneself appeals to one's goodness (see also Joldersma 2009a). The ethical interruptions involved in education unsettle not only one's personal striving for enjoyment, but also the very inward-directedness that is intrinsic to conatus. The ethical calls from others invite one's thoughtfulness to work on behalf of others, an appeal to a strange goodness within. Education involves calling attention to the goodness that might flow from oneself, with generosity. The spirit that animates education is an outward-directed distribution of responsibility across the network of relationships among humans, a continuous interruption of self-interested conatus with the goodness of one's concern for the welfare of others as other—those with whom one has little in common (see Joldersma 2009b). It turns out that the interruption required for understanding's development is also an entreaty to join others in being responsible for third parties, an appeal to one's goodness.

My interpretation of education is an attempt to see it as something basic to our humanity. As part of our primordial way of being human, education is intrinsic to understanding's functioning. At the same time education involves an originary ethical relation to the other, unsettling the self-directed character of the striving to live. And because of its social setting, the call of many others, education orients one to the social, to the call of justice.

References

Deakin Crick, R., & Joldersma, C. W. (2007). Habermas, lifelong learning and citizenship education. *Studies in Philosophy and Education, 26*(2), 77–95.

Joldersma, C. W. (2002). Pedagogy of the other: A Levinasian approach to the teacher-student relation. In S. Rice (Ed.), *Philosophy of education society yearbook 2001*. Urbana, IL: Philosophy of Education Society-University of Illinois.

Joldersma, C. W. (2005). Incarnate being and Carnal knowledge: The caress beyond the grasp. In J. H. Kok (Ed.), *Ways of knowing: In concert*. Sioux Center, IA: Dordt College Press.

Joldersma, C. W. (2006). Not only what or how, but who? Subjectivity, obligation and the call to teach. *Journal of Education and Christian Belief, 10*(1), 61–73.

Joldersma, C. W. (2008a). The importance of enjoyment and inspiration for learning from a teacher. In D. Egéa-Kuehne (Ed.), *Levinas and education: At the intersection of faith and reason* (pp. 43–55). London & New York: Routledge.

Joldersma, C. W. (2008b). Beyond rational autonomy: Levinas and the incomparable worth of the student as singular other. *Interchange, 39*(1), 21–47.

Joldersma, C. W. (2009a). Ethics, justice, prophecy: Cultivating civic virtue from a Levinasian perspective. In R. D. Glass (Ed.), *Philosophy of education society yearbook 2008* (pp. 264–267). Urbana, IL: Philosophy of Education Society.

Joldersma, C. W. (2009b). A spirituality of the desert for education: The call of justice beyond the individual or community. *Studies in Philosophy and Education, 28*(3), 193–208.

Joldersma, C. W. (2009c). How can science help us care for nature? Hermeneutics, fragility and responsibility for the earth. *Educational Theory, 59*(4), 465–483.

Joldersma, C. W. (2011). Who is the teacher? Testimony, uniqueness and responsibility—response to Lorraine Code's 'particularity, epistemic responsibility, and the ecological imaginary. In G. J. Biesta (Ed.), *Philosophy of education society yearbook 2010* (pp. 35–38). Urbana, IL: Philosophy of Education Society & University of Illinois Press.

Joldersma, C. W., & Deakin Crick, R. (2010). Citizenship, discourse ethics and an emancipatory model of lifelong learning. In M. Murphy & T. Fleming (Eds.), *Habermas, critical theory and education* (pp. 137–152). London: Routledge.

Exercising Theory: A Perspective on its Practice

Christiane Thompson

Published online: 20 April 2011
© Springer Science+Business Media B.V. 2011

Abstract   What is the task of educational theory or philosophy if it is not merely conceived as specification of philosophical doctrines in the realm of education? In my view it is the particular task of educational-philosophical theory to *work critically on* the historically developed cultural constructs that shape our (educational) experience. Thus, the activity that educational theorists are to perform is the critical reflection of the "limits of our world" by drawing on philosophical references and theories. In this text I describe this activity drawing from my own research practice with a particular focus on its relation to what is called thinking.

Keywords   Educational theory · Research practice · Writing · Différance

The starting point of my reflection is the objection to an understanding of theory as a remote and introspective whole which has detached itself from that with which it is engaged. This conception of theory has repeatedly been problematized within the tradition of Western educational philosophy. Self-sufficient binary oppositions such as 'theory and praxis' and 'theory and empirical research' have been continually called into question. Adorno has e.g. time and again described thinking as an *act(ivity)* and theory as a *gestalt of practice*. As such, thinking is part of an activity that is able to change something about the world. Simply put: theory is a world-changing act.

Adorno's negative dialectics also distances itself from a conception of theory which defines itself in terms of its opposition to "empirical research". For Adorno it is not the structure or comparison of data and thought that is decisive; rather what is problematic is the manner in which identification is at work in the prevalent conceptions of both "theory" and "empirical research". This notion of identification is connected to a detached conception of method in which method remains external to the objects of study (to which it [method] is being applied). For Adorno the sterility of this methodological procedure

C. Thompson (✉)
Faculty of Philosophy III, Educational Sciences, Martin-Luther-University Halle-Wittenberg,
06099 Halle/Saale, Germany
e-mail: christiane.thompson@paedagogik.uni-halle.de

G. J. J. Biesta (ed.), *Making Sense of Education*, DOI: 10.1007/978-94-007-4017-4_4,   21
© Springer Science+Business Media Dordrecht 2012

cannot be productive in either a theoretical or empirical sense. Knowledge can only be generated in an activity where the limits of one's own approach become articulated. As such, theory constitutes a fragmented and self-reflexive undertaking.

My intention here is not to develop and defend a particular understanding of educational theory based on Adorno or any other philosophical figure. Thus, I do not want to provide "grounds for justification", which has been the mode of philosophical reflection since ancient philosophy: from the ancient Greek conception of *logon didonai* to Kant's epistemology as a critique of pure reason to Habermas' examination of validity claims to analytic philosophy's logical analysis. Philosophy has clearly held on to the demarcation between that what is justified and what is not, even when the line has been drawn very differently by various theoretical traditions. Moreover, it is not a question whether solid argumentation is a virtue—some even view it as the essential or defining philosophical characteristic within educational theory. And while I will not, in what follows, be dealing with "grounds for justification", this nevertheless does not mean that thinking and thought are excluded from my consideration.

The aim here is not to advance yet another "understanding" among many other approaches to theory to be argued for and possibly established. When I say that theory has little to do with a detached attitude, the question I am primarily interested in is related to that *what we do* when we exercise theory. In other words, I will examine this form of activity and, as such, expand the perspective of theory in its concreteness.

The importance of this kind of analysis and work is due to the recent and increasingly frequent association of educational theory as so-called "foundational research" within the educational sciences. The transfer of the concept from the natural sciences implies that pedagogical theory exists for itself, that it is something detached from social practices and thus from pedagogical practices. Is an educational-philosophical approach like the 15th decimal place of the gravitational constant? The transfer of the concept from the natural sciences also implies that there is something like *fundamentals* or *basic principles* in education, i.e. immutable and uniform points of reference standing in contrast to their "real-world counterparts". The concept of "foundational research" is part of a nomenclature that relegates theory to self-referential reflection, a place without the world. Correspondingly, "empirical research" is conceived as a mode of investigation that fully "engages" with the world, e.g. by providing governing knowledge within the educational system.

It is precisely such conceptual usages that stand in opposition to an elaborated notion of theory in relation to practice and empirical research. Perspectives and terminologies generate reality: They sketch out the educational field and contain certain tacit priorities. For this reason, I am interested in examining that which we often lose sight of when we conceive of theory simply as an available and objective foundation. The point of departure here is my impression that in the exercise of theory the activity is "extinguished" in order to make the result of this activity present, namely the "theory". I will elaborate this thought by looking more closely at the question of method; for it is method—in the "modern" sense—that guarantees the possibility of extinguishing the subjects' research activities. In other words, method enables an understanding of the scientific result as something which can be represented as detached or independent of the researcher's activity.

A critical analysis of method not only clarifies the process of the autonomization of knowledge in the modern period (i.e. its detachment from a truth-guaranteeing entity such as God), but at the same time constitutes a leitmotif allowing us to examine more closely the practice of theorizing. Descartes' proclamation "clare et distincte" can still be said to characterize all scientific endeavors. That which is not clear and distinct—thus intersub-jectively comprehensible—cannot be deemed "knowledge", and thus remains mere belief. Corresponding to the methodological extinction of the research process is the inter-sub-jective validity-directed abstinence and self-discipline of the researcher.

However, to exercise theory means, as I will work out in the following, that we con-struct a relationship to the objects that we thematize, and that we also build a relationship to this practice—which includes a relationship to ourselves. These relationships to the issues and to us engaging with them cannot be made explicit in knowledge; for they are dependent on the subject and cannot be deducted from them. I will pursue this dimension of the "subjective" by shedding some light on several practices of doing or exercising theory. Applying a reflective view and carrying out a self-description, I will look at the practices of *underlining*, *contemplation* and *writing*.

Underlining is a widespread practice commonly accompanying the reading of texts. When I read, I let myself become part of what is read and expose myself to the text. However, reading does not occur in a linear fashion, and the connection to what is read is not consistent. The process of underlining is an activity by means of which I am able (besides deciding what is relevant) to *hold on to my own reading*. The line I draw is a manifestation of this relationship. The underlined text represents an accentuation which later re-iterates my attention. It is quite common that my reading is already directed by a particular question that guides it and to which my intonations are already aligned. Moreover, I sometimes jot something down in the page margin thus placing my own writing next to the text.

To perform this reading—a reading that does not become invisible—is the first step to that what is called thinking. In other words, when we begin to think, in fact, something dialogical is present—a duplication of the text, which represents an opening of oneself to the speech of the Other who is not present. In this sense we are not only concerned with the meaning and validity of "a text"—which one could claim represents a unity. Rather, the "text" is a virtual instrument that enables the reader to enter into a kind of relation to oneself—above all in the case where I attempt to remain *true* to a text.

Underlining provides me with concepts, fragments of thoughts, and even possibly arguments that outline the contours and shape of an issue. This outlining is not reducible to the construction of a body of knowledge or systematic thought. Because I do not attribute the underlining to myself, but rather the absent Other, I understand it as a caesura with what I previously understood. Reading unfolds itself around a difference of "thinking-this-way-and-otherwise", a difference that the text already embodies. In our "listening", our dispossession in exposition (Heidegger: *Hörigkeit*), we yield or give ourselves over to what we have read, whose polyphony is collected in reading.

The second practice that I will present is a form of *contemplation*. To be sure, this practice is associated with explorative forms of reading. When I, for example, read Der-rida's "A certain Impossible Possibility of saying the Event", I make my reading visible. This, in turn, leads me to reflect on the category of the "impossible possibility". In the practice of contemplation the various perspectives are brought together in order to ask how the object under consideration is identified, is referred to, and finally how this category "a certain impossible possibility of saying the event" is to be understood.

I consider such a condensation of the reading to be an essential moment of exercising theory because the issue to be observed and determined is viewed *in a variety of ways*. The issue detaches itself from a particular course or line of thought and starts to call upon innumerable reference points. By means of this, the issue takes up the quality of a *thing*—forming a conglomeration of irreducible perspectives and thus delineating the borders of our thinking. In such situations the determination of the issue is exacerbated. Not only are various points of reference in the sense of different dimensions of explanation or theories invoked, but the issue takes up various categorical functions.

For example, Derrida's "impossible possibility" is part of a self-reflection that addresses the inaccessibility of the relationship to oneself (e.g. with regard to the "gift"). At the same time, it acts as a critical re-situation of Western philosophy, which always understood possibility as an optional availability and never in terms of impossibility. Eventually, Derrida endues the "impossible possibility" with a gesture alluding to the receptivity for the unknowable Other. As I see it, Derrida's category is relevant for educational theory because thinking the "possibility" is an integral part of every pedagogical process. This is due to the fact that education and *Bildung* are primarily concerned with the "not yet", but what *could come to be*. By moving the question of education and *Bildung* closer to Derrida's complex categorical figures, thinking becomes alienating and is experienced as resistance; for learning and educating represent exactly these relationships of ego and the Other—relationships that we commonly spell out in terms of conceptions of possibility as "option" or "alternative": "I can explain Foucault's concept of assemblage to students taking 'possibility A' or 'possibility B', etc.". In such thinking the possibility and what is to be done—the explanation of a concept—remain indifferent to one another. What happens, for instance, when the category of possibility becomes alienating? Rancière's thinking in "The Ignorant Schoolmaster" began precisely at this point, by asking how the *possibility of explanation* in educational relationships should be understood and what explanation implies for the listener.

As such, I 'perform' contemplation for the purpose of alienation, an uncertainty or multiplicity of what I had previously thought. By alienation I mean here the dissolution of the familiarity with an issue or object. This loss of familiarity can arise when competing and apparently incompatible perspectives of an issue are placed next to each other. A sudden shift or even intensification of perspective can also result in such a loss of familiarity. Here, I would like to introduce a further example.

When I reflect upon Adorno's often contemplated and widely discussed dictum "The premier demand upon all education is that Auschwitz not happen again", it is still possible that it draws the reader or listener into a deep alienation. The reason for this is that Adorno introduces a statement determining a theoretical concept (education) and, at the same time, he closes off the idea of conceptual determination: Adorno rejects conceptual determination and fills the concept of education with the *incomparable* Auschwitz. Adorno's *conceptual statement* presents the breakdown of education as a *concept*. What could education then be? Is a question like this one (from present to future) even possible? How can we talk about education after the insight that the theoretical engagement with it, not to mention its achievements rooted in the Enlightenment, were unable to prevent the incomparable horrors of the Holocaust? On the contrary, the idealized form of education, the self-confidence of humanism contributed to the catastrophic events. What do I think in this very moment?

The third practice that I will introduce, *writing*, represents to an extent the closure of alienation, even when conflict and resistance—as they are present in contemplation—are brought into the writing. Writing, which is not to be confused with what is written, is an activity, a committing of oneself to following a thought as well as its obligational force. I place certain things in the foreground and thereby fix other thoughts as points of departure or as presuppositions. I give myself over to a particular self-directed train of thought. This train of thought is not just a collection of whatever is present at hand, but rather that which is also characterized by an eventfulness and the fateful determination of this process.

Regardless of whether we continually revise what has been written, we cannot extinguish the performative quality connected to it.

A text that attempts to control everything and penetrates into the objecthood of the issues via a totality of perspective would most likely have *said* a great many things but is actually *saying* very little. In writing we exist at a limit. This limit does not just consist of the limitation of space to be filled or the limitation of time: All writing must eventually come to an end in order to *release* the text. Notably, I am always already at the limit in the process of writing because I must continually make myself into a reader: I read what has been written, and in so doing I read it differently. Perhaps I begin to underline, to contemplate in order to write anew—to write differently.

At the heart of a text taking shape lies a history of thinking, which, in order to become a text, becomes invisible. To be more specific, one cannot really speak of a finished text in terms of a "result". There is nothing to read where reading does not occur, and thus qua *différance* will always be read differently: where the text gets under way and changes in the Other's thinking.

Looking back at the various practices that I have described in a preliminary analysis, we may be estranged by conceptions of theory as constellations or totalities of sentences. There is so much more taking place when moving (not only between but) within the lines. Theory as totality does not grasp the activities and practices of thinking. This conglomeration of practices, which in my opinion possess philosophical qualities, does not remain external to how I see myself in what I do. *Underlining, contemplation,* and *writing* all move within a field of difference between understanding and not-understanding. All of these practices can be considered *translations* in which the difference between understanding and not-understanding is set in motion; a movement in which we approach ourselves by means of the Other's voice and make ourselves speak.

What is it that I want to say here without bringing knowledge into the equation? I will follow up with a few remarks regarding the task of "theory" in the pedagogical and the educational field as I understand it.

It is relatively easy to portray the generation of theory concerning pedagogical processes when the underlying categories are clearly defined. Where "education" is measured referring to a state of knowledge or in view of defined tasks that are organized and rated according to their probability of solution, there exists a clear categorical make-up of the underlying pedagogical processes. This categorical structure may e.g. be differentiated according to different levels of competence. To be sure, in the process of constructing competence models conceptual problems can emerge. However, these models are not concerned with the categorical make-up of "education"; for here it has already been decided that we are dealing with constructs of a *capacity* that is attributable to a subject.

The category "education" or "*Bildung*" starts to lose its grip when we regard education or *Bildung* as an individual comportment or attitude. Since it is the individual's task to understand and disclose its history and identity according to (socially mediated) references of meaning and human action, every moment bears the difficulty of its identification. One such example might be the refusal of a person to open herself to the idea of life-long learning. What does this refusal mean for the educational dimension of this person's life? Who is in a position to decide whether this attitude might be considered a learning experience or the decision of its impossibility? To whom do we want to attribute the conceptual power to decide? It is anything but easy to judge the educational significance of experience as the example of Socrates shows: In the Platonic dialogues, he sought to demonstrate to his interlocutors that a close connection exists between ignorance and education, i.e. in the recognition of the limits of one's own ability to know. The question of education and *Bildung* becomes fascinating and challenging when the standards by which one could decide upon educational processes are also called into question.

It is the task of educational philosophy to reflect upon the categorical make-up of pedagogical processes. This includes the determination of pedagogical concepts such as "education", "Bildung", "learning", "teaching" etc. Moreover, the reflective work extends to other categorical dimensions of education, e.g. "possibility" (see above) or "temporality". Here, the linear logic of temporality and presence as it is widely understood in the progression of pedagogical processes—"beginning, process, end" or "pre-condition, performance, future prospects"—can be called into question.

Educational theorists concerned with categorical questions *work on* historically developed cultural constructs (such as the temporality of *Bildung* as experience or the relationship of education and power). More precisely, educational theorists are not merely executors of philosophical doctrines in the realm of education: They do not just figure out the topics and then arrive at a conclusion, e.g. the *result* when one brings together the modern concept of education with Kierkegaard. The particular activity that educational theorists are to perform is in my view the critical reflection of the "limits of our world" by drawing on philosophical references and theories. The "limits of our world" are in turn related to the approval of those categories that constitute our experience. This activity is critical and perhaps even deconstructive because it discloses the borders of our experience.

By exposing the difference between understanding and not-understanding, as I have described above, the horizons of possibility involving the constitution of pedagogically meaningful experience are critically evaluated. It should have become clear that I do not conceive of theoretical work as a self-complacent enterprise that operates from a comfortable distance. The critical self-confrontation that takes place in thinking refers as much to the work at the "limits of the world" as at the "limits of subject"; for they pertain equally to conditions under which we consider ourselves to be a "learning" or "knowledgeable" subject or even a 'researcher'.

That we today conceive of theoretical work in terms of a self-referential framework, as a body of knowledge, as a systematic ensemble of sentences, etc. is connected to the revaluation and appreciation of method as well as the autonomization of knowledge in the modern era. What is forgotten in this context is a rich tradition that viewed theorizing as being connected with a *form of life* and a *work on oneself* (see for example Stoa). By focusing on knowledge, on the text, and on the valid proposition, we lose sight of the philosophical and scientific task to reflect upon how we see things and whether we could see them differently.

Lived Relationality as Fulcrum for Pedagogical–Ethical Practice

Tone Saevi

Published online: 20 April 2011
© Springer Science+Business Media B.V. 2011

Abstract What is the core of pedagogical practice? Which qualities are primary to the student–teacher relationship? What is a suitable language for pedagogical practice? What might be the significance of an everyday presentational pedagogical act like for example the glance of a teacher? The pedagogical relation as lived relationality experientially sensed, as well as phenomenologically described and interpreted, precedes educational methods and theories and profoundly challenges educational practice and reflection. The paper highlights the aporetic character of pedagogical practice, reflection and research by suggesting that the pedagogical relation opens up for a practice that is ethically and existentially normative rather than developmentally and socially normative, and thus fundamentally shifts the meaning of education.

Keywords Hermeneutic phenomenology · Relation · Ethics · Continental pedagogy · Existential pedagogy

Introduction

The phenomenological and existential European pedagogy at the core of this paper can perhaps best be introduced not through common historical or theoretical conceptions, but through a particular vibrant description told by a young learning-disabled student named Oda:

> When my answer is wrong, I know it immediately because Per [the teacher] looks at me with this particular humorous glance and says, after just a little pause: "Yes...?" Then I understand that he wants me to give the question a second thought. He just

T. Saevi (✉)
NLA University College, Bergen, Norway
e-mail: ts@nla.no

leans back comfortably and waits. That's why I like him so much. I feel relaxed and smart with him.[1]

The gentle gesture that opens up to Oda a sense of approval and respect is the teacher's glance and his serene and trustful dwelling with her. The glance Oda and her teacher exchanges is not a reciprocal glance, as if they were equals and the teacher had the right to expect something in return. The teacher's glance "grants a kind of space and a set of possibilities for Oda without any expectations that these will be granted in return" (Friesen and Saevi 2010, p. 124). The teacher's glance practices a certain caring forgetfulness to Oda's learning disability and is sensitive to her latent sense of inferiority and vulnerable sense of self. The glance recognizes Oda in a way that seems to comply with how she in the moment sees herself; as a person with learning difficulties that is in need of a second chance, but also as a person with ability worthy of the trust of a teacher. Oda's lived sense of self is strengthened and encouraged by this particular glance.

However, the situation Oda describes is likely not an isolated incidence. The teacher seems to be willing to go through several situations of the same kind in order to offer the student a new chance every time. The teacher's glance lets the student experience the look as enabling and encouraging, somehow "knowing" whether to see infirmity or not. Herein lies the pedagogical paradox of seeing students. The pedagogical glance practices a certain willed passing over, a caring "blindness" that is significant as to what it sees and not sees. The pedagogical glance, the way this teacher practices it, is forgetful or protectively blind to infirmity and disability, and constantly strives to strengthen and enable the student, by acknowledging and recognizing her but at the same time passing over what should not be called attention to (Saevi 2005, p. 164). Oda recalls a moment that stands out for her and gives the teacher the credit for her sense of approval. The moment might seem insignificant and lead into other seemingly trivial moments in everyday events in school, but to Oda the experience of self was at stake and the teacher's immediate tactful gesture recognized this in her and responded responsibly to the situation.

"Seeing" as a Pedagogical Act

Oda's account of how she is being given the opportunity to see herself as a capable and agreeable student has previously introduced two papers of mine (Saevi and Eilifsen 2008; Friesen and Saevi 2010). The pedagogical richness of the account however, renders it possible to lift out aspects significant also to the focus of this paper. As pedagogy is understood in the phenomenological and existentially oriented European tradition one may say that the teacher's glance is an exemplary pedagogical *act* that strives toward the good of the child and young person (Friesen and Saevi 2010). The pedagogical act of seeing students presupposes educational practice as well as theoretical considerations and methods, and is, like Oda's account speaks to, a pedagogical relationality recognized experientially by the person who is being seen (or not seen). From experience we know that being seen by someone is different from seeing someone, yet this simple insight, like our sense of self, somehow is too close to us to be recognized as a relational precondition for pedagogical practice (Saevi 2005, p. 63).

---

[1] This description is taken from a collection of interviews from 2001 to 2002 with intellectually disabled high school students in Norway that are described, translated and referenced in (Saevi 2005). The names are pseudonyms.

The complex act of seeing someone is immediate, as well as pre-comprehensive and even biased, but in the very moment of seeing our glance is intertwined with and interdependent to action. Seeing as an instant pedagogical act presupposes and differs from pedagogical reflection of what to focus on and how to see students. How we see someone, either for the first time or repeatedly, is always ahead of how we act. Thus seeing as a way of interpreting the world is the beginning of action and reflection, because the way we see is the way the world appears to us and the precondition of how we act and of what we reflect upon. How teachers see students and their lifeworlds is crucial to students and to pedagogical practice by the very fact that perception, or seeing, never is a "deliberate taking up of a position" (Merleau-Ponty 1945/2002, p. xi). Seeing someone or something is the basis and condition of all action and, as such, always includes some sort of understanding and interpretation (Gadamer 1965/1985). One might say that the pedagogical act of seeing somehow unites the seer and the seen, while paradoxically also separating them, precisely in that seeing and being seen is sensed differently by the two persons. How teachers see is related to who and how he or she is in the world, and to their relationships to their students. Likewise, how the student experiences being seen relates to his or her lived self and the relationship to the teacher. There seem to be ways of seeing students that are more pedagogically valuable to the persons being seen than others; like for example the sensitivity of the glance of Oda's teacher and its appropriateness to how Oda senses herself in the moment as well as when she later on recalls the vital moment.

One may ask, however, if the attentive recognition that Oda experiences from her teacher is what really counts for her. Is the pedagogical glance that strives for the good of each student primary to the student–teacher relationship, or is it just a bonus? Considering lived pedagogical–ethical relationality as primary to education profoundly disturbs the didactic procedure of providing and receiving educational knowledge as a routine or procedural process. Education is often primarily understood as a set of personal or political ideas or ways of organizing students in learning institutions, or as a well-articulated cultural philosophy aiming at preparing the younger generation for a changing future. However, phenomenological and existential pedagogy first and foremost sees education as intentional relational practice resting on ethical pedagogy, and directed towards the uniquely experienced life of the child and young person, to support the entire personal life and life experience of this person. The available scene is our everyday life with children, where children and adults, students and teachers, meet, relate, communicate, and interact in institutions and situations of many kinds. Every encounter is unique, unrepeatable and called into being by the present persons, for a purpose, and within a context. Yet, these child–adult, student–teacher encounters have something in common. For one, the relationship is asymmetric in that the two sides' intent, authority, responsibility and role differ. The encounter typically has some kind of purpose, such as upbringing, teaching, guiding or supervising. Besides, the relationship often includes some kind of care offered by, or included in the actions of, the adult, although the quality and mode of the care might vary, depending on the purpose of the relation, the adult's ability to care, the age of the child and the experienced need for care. The caring act, as well as the pedagogical relation as such, are intentionally turned towards the good of the child and would otherwise not be called care or pedagogy. Pedagogy thus primarily is not a term that *indicates* the relation between adult and child as an educational representation, but rather pedagogy is a certain existentially charged togetherness that *creates or lets grow* something presentationally and personally between them, something of a lasting, although often smoldering quality.

Mollenhauer (1983) echoing Nohl (1970) sees the relation between adult and child as the origin and the only possible starting point of educational practice. Along with other previous and contemporary European pedagogues like Johann H. Pestalozzi (1807), Otto F. Bollnow (1960, 1989), Max van Manen (1991, 1997) and Wilfried Lippitz (1990, 2007), Mollenhauer understands the adult's thoughtful responsiveness toward the child's subjective life and life experience as the inherent pedagogic qualities in educational practice. These qualities are pedagogically possible and productive only as relational qualities between adult and child, teacher and student. The relation rests on the asymmetric, tactful and personal togetherness that is deeply grounded in the difference between the generations and the personal and cultural need for upbringing and education.

Even though we have all been children and this particular life experience belongs to us all, our familiarity with what it is like to be a child must take on the form of recollection for adults. However, artists, such as painters or poets, somehow in their work protect childhood and keep memory traces alive in our culture; although their ever so vibrant and recognizable works are still only representations of the real lived experience that took place in the past. Lived childhood experience unalterably is beyond your reach because the very moment of the experience belongs to the past. Somehow being a child is also protected by the uniqueness of each child's experience as well as the immediateness of each situation. Lived experience as life experience thus comes to mean something else to the child than to adult or to the grown child. As adults through the course of time, our grown-up-ness prevents us from seeing and from being aware of the child's vulnerability when the qualities of the adult world meet the child's experiential world (Saevi and Husevaag 2009). Children are in the situations of life in their own ways—ways and manners that adults, if they are fortunate, see as recognizable traces. Traces rather than evidence of how the particular child experiences the world leaves us with the possibility of a pedagogical relation, as the child is both visible and invisible to us. The otherness of each child, as well as the adults' foreignness to childhood as lifeworld experience, are qualities of the human life condition that cannot be overcome by pedagogical endeavor, being it relationship, professional educational knowledge, control or constant surveillance. The pedagogical relation is characterized by being an impasse, and can only exist as a possibility that may evolve in each new encounter between adult and child. The pedagogical caring and thoughtful relationship between the adult and child gets its intrinsic life and energy from the tension of the opposite: the utter uniqueness and inaccessibility of the child's self and lifeworld. Paradoxically this is the pedagogical opportunity that renders possible the pedagogical relationship (p. 35).

The pedagogical relation exists in the shade of our everyday life with children, and is practiced within the impasse of sameness and otherness. As teachers we anticipate conformity as well as uniqueness from the child, a condition that calls for alternatives and responsible being and doing in pedagogical settings. The potentiality of the pedagogical relation challenges its ethical base and pedagogical intent, and distinguishes the pedagogic from the non-pedagogic in the very moment of the relation (Saevi 2005). Even more significantly, if the relation between the adult and the child should be interpreted as a *pedagogical* relation, the pedagogical and the ethical are not only intertwined, but have never been separate (Saevi 2007, p. 126). The overriding and constant dilemma of the pedagogical relation is how to practice a pedagogy that is sufficiently aware of the imperfection and profound openness of each unique child, in order not to end in consuming or limiting its foreignness. Can we protect the pedagogical qualities by not making the child an equal of the teacher and someone they already know? Unfortunately, as adults we cannot step outside the constraints of socialization and conventions, or of our self-centred striving for sameness and synchronization of views and wills, and decide to overcome these constraints and become successful parents and teachers. What we can do, however, is constantly to try to be attentive to the experience of the child and to acknowledge the child's utter otherness as the basis and precondition of pedagogical relational practice (Saevi and Husevaag 2009, p. 40).

Language is a Passageway

Like beauty can be the passage to truth, according to Heidegger (1971/2001), p. 54), language guides our practice of upbringing and education. However, language, unlike beauty, often passes unnoticed as a handy tool for practice. The language of pedagogical practice though, speaks in anecdotes, stories, examples and questions that provide opportunity for experience rather than explanation, for listening rather than verification (Saevi 2010, p. 2). The language which speaks of education both is a unification of what is said and an authorization of the person speaking, and thus is significant to concrete practice. Today typically psychological and instrumental ways of thinking are given powerful expression in the psychologically dominated vocabulary commonplace in discussions of education and development. This is a vocabulary that has become ever more professionalized and instrumentalised, with the "non-specialized" meanings of older terms either being gradually re-defined or replaced with terms or meanings that are specialized, and instrumentally or psychologically charged (Friesen and Saevi 2010). The word *education* itself provides a good example. Originally referring to the general "process of nourishing or rearing a child or young person", this term has increasingly come to refer to what happens exclusively in the school, namely the "systematic instruction, schooling or training given to the young" (Old English Dictionary (OED)). Erziehung, the closest German equivalent to education provides an alternative example. Erziehung can be translated as "breeding, "education", or "upbringing", blurring the boundary between school and home, personal and professional (Friesen and Saevi 2010). The meanings and availability and unavailability of specialized educational vocabularies within psychology, biology and means-ends rationality in general, lead effectively but almost imperceptibly to certain ways of thinking, speaking, and writing that can be difficult but valuable to retrace and reconsider (p. 126). Education has become a specialized term of psychologically charged methods and a distinct focus on self-improvement, while Erziehung belongs to a culture where pedagogical practice was influenced by the unspecialized language of questions and uncertainties that in itself encloses an emphasis on existential ways of being and acting. Here the "tasks and responsibilities of teaching are no longer framed by essentialistic definitions of the ontologenetic and phylogenetic provided by psychology [...] but are seen as emerging from a sustained encounter between generations, specifically between a particular adult or teacher and a particular child or student as persons" (p. 142). If language has the ability to let practice happen, or to help us see and practice the "isness" of pedagogical practice, what then is the suitable language for education seen as a potential pedagogical relational practice?

A suitable language for which Mollenhauer and we as pedagogues search should be seen both as a literal language of educational research and the language presented and represented by the teacher in the classroom. However, this unspecialized language also is the "language" in the sense of visual, cinematic and narrative or fictive languages (p. 127). An unspecialized language is inherently concrete, tangible, detailed and situated to events, settings, relations and persons. Fiction, painting and film address us personally and compellingly and thus have an "intrinsic portability or "translatability" across cultures" (p. 142). Languages like these are existential and mantic[2]-expressive and have the potential of addressing teachers and students personally in transformative ways non-cognitively as well as cognitively. The unspecialized language speaks to our lived understanding that is less cognitive than we tend to believe. Lived understanding rather is intertwined in our relational existence, because simply "by living one's life and by reflecting on existence, we bring life out of concealedness by living its intentional meaning" (Henriksson and Saevi 2009, p. 41).

The Aporetic Character of Pedagogy

The pedagogical relation is the existential ethical basis of pedagogical practice and its intention and qualities are conditions sustaining that the relationship between the child and the adult is a pedagogical relationship and not another kind of relation among the variety of sorts of human relationships. The existential condition though, also "entails an acute awareness of the limitations of this approach to pedagogy" (Friesen and Saevi 2010, p. 142) as the absence of certainties, formulas and methods, exchanged by the pedagogical relation impress upon us the paradoxical and aporetic character of pedagogy. Mollenhauer notices the need for this aporetic quality when he says, "The more finely the net of pedagogical strategies and institutions is woven, the greater a contribution that is expected from pedagogy toward social progress, the more difficult it becomes to validate this" [aporetic character] (1983, p. 88). Pedagogy is aporetic to Mollenhauer in that it tries to describe and strengthen the fundamentally open and indefinite child about whom nothing final or decisive can be said. The profoundly personal and ethical relation between adult and child that cannot be defined in specialized language is a relation intended to guide and support each child's way towards humanity and selfhood.

In conclusion, for the existential phenomenological approach to education, with its prioritization of concrete existence over abstract essence, the pedagogical relation can be described as situationally and ethically normative rather than developmentally and socially normative (Friesen and Saevi 2010, p. 140). The notion of education as an unspecialized practice; as a way of simply and authentically "being with" children means that it is not principally a matter of enumerable set of skills and competences, which are (or are not) one's possession. Pedagogy is instead a question of who and how one *is* in relation to children. It is a matter of one's disposition, one's personal, physical and emotional presence or presentation, of one's personal relationship with *this* particular child (p. 143). The paradoxical and at the same time differentiating qualities of the pedagogical relation radically shift the meaning of education by ethically challenging the lived relationality of each encounter between adult and child, teacher and student.

References

Bollnow, O. F. (1960). *Neue Geborgenheit. Das Problem einer Überwindung Existentialismus.* Stuttgart: W. Kohlhammer.

---

[2] From Greek *mantikos*, from *mantis* lit. "one who divines, a seer, prophet," from *mainesthai* "be inspired," related to *menos* "passion, spirit. Etymology Dictionary, available online at: http://www.etymonline.com/.

Bollnow, O. F. (1989). The pedagogical atmosphere. *Phenomenology + Pedagogy 7.*

Friesen, N., & Saevi, T. (2010). Reviving forgotten connections in North American teacher education: Klaus Mollenhauer and the pedagogical relation. *Journal of Curriculum Studies, 42*(1), 123–147.

Gadamer, H-G. (1965/1985). *Truth and method.* New York: Crossroad.

Heidegger, M. (1971/2001). *Poetry, language, thought.* New York: Harper & Row.

Henriksson, C., & Saevi, T. (2009). "An event in sound". Considerations on the ethical- aesthetic traits of the hermeneutic phenomenological text. *Phenomenology & Practice, 3*(1), 35–58.

Lippitz, W. (1990). Ethics as limits of pedagogical reflection. *Phenomenology + Pedagogy, 8,* 49–60.

Lippitz, W. (2007). Foreignness and otherness in the pedagogical context. *Phenomenology & Practice, 1*(1), 79–96.

Merleau-Ponty, M. (1945/2002). *Phenomenology of perception.* London: Routledge.

Mollenhauer, K. (1983). *Vergessene Zusammenhänge.* Über Kultur und Erziehung. München: Juventa.

Nohl, H. (1970). *Die Pädagogische Bewegung in Deutschland und Ihre Theorie.* Frankfurt a: M G. Schulte– Bulmke.

Pestalozzi, J. H. (1807). Letter from Pestalozzi to a friend on his work at Stanz. Available online at: http://elearn.tru.ca/index.php/Letter_from_Pestalozzi_to_a_friend_on_his_work_at_Stanz.

Saevi, T. (2005). *Seeing disability pedagogically: The lived experience of disability in the pedagogical encounter.* Bergen: Bergen University Press.

Saevi, T. (2007). Den pedagogiske relasjonen, en relasjon annerledes enn andre relasjoner [The pedagogical relation, a relation different from other relations]. In O. H. Kaldestad et al. (Eds.)Bergen: Fagbokforlaget (pp. 107–131), *Grunnverdier og pedagogikk. [Basic Values and Education].*

Saevi, T. (2010). Editorial. *Phenomenology & Practice, 4*(1), 1–4.

Saevi, T., & Eilifsen, M. (2008). 'Heartful' or 'heartless' teachers? Or should we look for the good somewhere else? Considerations of students' experience of the pedagogical good. *Indo-Pacific Journal of Phenomenology, 8,* 1–14.

Saevi, T., & Husevaag, H. (2009). The child seen as the same or the other? The significance of the social convention to the pedagogical relation. *Paideusis, 18*(2), 29–41.

Van Manen, M. (1991). *The tact of teaching.* Ontario: The Althouse Press.

Van Manen, M. (1997). *Researching lived experience. Human science for an action sensitive pedagogy.* Ontario: The Althouse Press.

Edwin & Phyllis

Lynn Fendler

Published online: 22 April 2011
© Springer Science+Business Media B.V. 2011

Abstract   Edwin, a person contemplating a career in teaching, has a conversation with Phyllis, a teacher and amateur theorist, about reasons to become a teacher.

Keywords   Teaching · Educational theory · Philosophy · Ethics · Democracy

Persons of the Dialogue:

PHYLLIS, a teacher and amateur theorist
EDWIN, a person who is contemplating a teaching career

Scene:

The House of Teac in the middle of the West

> EDWIN: I'm thinking of becoming a teacher.
> PHYLLIS: Oh, why?
> EDWIN: Because I love children.
> PHYLLIS: I see. Do you know of any person who does not love children?
> EDWIN: Well, unfortunately there are people who abuse or neglect children.
> PHYLLIS: Yes, and tragically there are children in the world who suffer miserably. Would you agree that people who willingly abuse or neglect children are sociopaths?
> EDWIN: Yes, of course.

L. Fendler (✉)
Department of Teacher Education, Michigan State University, 362 Erickson Hall, East Lansing, MI 48823, USA
e-mail: fendler@msu.edu

L. Fendler
Faculty of Language and Literature, Humanities, Arts and Educational Sciences, Campus Walferdange, Batiment III, 01.002, Route de Diekirch, 7220 Walferdange, Luxembourg

PHYLLIS: And, obviously we agree that sociopaths should never become teachers. But other than sociopaths, it's perhaps universal that people love children. Do you mean to imply that anyone other than a sociopath has a good reason to become a teacher?

EDWIN: No, I guess not. When you put it that way, I guess loving children is not sufficient reason to become a teacher.

PHYLLIS: So it seems. Do you have any other reasons for wanting to become a teacher?

EDWIN: Yes. I really love mathematics and art. I would like to share my love of mathematics and art with other people.

PHYLLIS: If you love mathematics and art, why don't you become a mathematician or artist?

EDWIN: Well, I suppose that would be one way to go. But wouldn't it be great to share my passion for these subjects so that other people can enjoy them and experience the sense of gratification that mathematics and art give us?

PHYLLIS: Certainly there are people who thoroughly enjoy mathematics and art, but they probably don't need teachers to encourage them in those pursuits. However, not everyone enjoys intellectual life. In fact, most people are not interested in studying; they prefer more practical kinds of work. Very few people choose academic careers, and even some professors are not happy, even though they are paid to be intellectuals. Do you think teachers should turn people into academics or try to persuade others to love a subject?

EDWIN: Not exactly. Teachers should offer people a chance to experience new subjects so students can decide for themselves what kind of work they like, but it's probably not a teacher's job to push people to enjoy intellectual life or to turn them into university types.

PHYLLIS: Then we agree that love for subject matter is not sufficient reason to become a teacher. Do you have any other reasons?

EDWIN: Yes, in fact, I do. I also want to make a difference in the world. I would like to give back to my community, to help make society a better place.

PHYLLIS: I admire your heartfelt commitment to serve the public good. In general, would you say our society is basically fair and equitable?

EDWIN: No! According to law, all people are supposed to have equal rights. But in reality, the fact is that rich people have easier access to better education than poor people have. So in that respect, the system is not equitable or just. Across demographic groups there are deplorable inequities in degrees of access to basic resources and quality education. These huge gaps signal fundamental injustices in our society.

PHYLLIS: You have an admirable social conscience! Do we agree then that our existing society, including the education system, is fundamentally unjust?

EDWIN: We agree that the injustices in our society are reprehensible. But are you saying that we need to have a revolution instead of better education?

PHYLLIS: That's not what I said. I'm just asking, since you are the product of an unjust system, and teachers work within that unjust system, in what way does that give you good reason to become a teacher? If you want to "give back to your community," it seems that you would have to transform the system, wouldn't you?

EDWIN: Yes. We have to transform the system to make society equitable and just for everyone.

PHYLLIS: But why do you think that becoming a teacher would be an effective way to do that? You might remember the words of the poet: "The master's tools will never dismantle the master's house."

EDWIN: I'm aware that it would be difficult for one teacher—especially one novice teacher—to have an impact on the system. Also, I don't necessarily have the leadership skills or experience to transform a whole education system. I would have to do a lot of things that are not your typical "teaching" in order to have an impact on society.

PHYLLIS: In that case, what kind of educational preparation would you need to help you accomplish your goal of changing the system?

EDWIN: Well, in order to have any effect on changing the school system, I'd certainly have to have more than pedagogical content knowledge. I'd need leadership training as a political activist. I'd have to study ethics and power, governmental processes, history, and mechanisms of social transformation. I would also need to have strong communication and technology skills. I can see that traditional teacher education isn't sufficient preparation if my goal is to have an impact on the fundamental injustices of society. But as a teacher I could at least have an effect on my classroom.

PHYLLIS: There are some heroic teachers who have performed miracles in their classrooms. I wish there were more teachers like that! But the contributions of those extraordinary teachers have not had an effect on the school system as a whole. Schools have consistently operated as institutions of reproduction and stratification in spite of repeated efforts by many people to reform them.

EDWIN: Hard to argue against that. You're right that even when teachers accomplish amazing feats in their own classrooms, I really cannot point to examples from history, research, or my experience that teachers have had an effect on the system. Regrettably, I have to agree that there's no evidence to suggest that teachers can have that kind of system-wide impact. I guess that's not sufficient reason to become a teacher, either.

PHYLLIS: Sad, but true.

EDWIN: Okay, I can see what you mean. But, really, you can't deny that teachers can make a difference. I had a teacher once who changed my life by believing in me and encouraging me. That's a good reason to become a teacher.

PHYLLIS: I hope that teacher received recognition and appreciation! In general, how many people's lives have been improved because of education?

EDWIN: It's true that, statistically speaking, education hasn't made much of a difference in the overall picture; widespread socioeconomic inequalities have remained basically unchanged.

PHYLLIS: That has historically been true. On rare occasions, education changes people's lives, but those cases are few and far between. Despite the fact that more and more people around the world have access to education, basic resources are still not fairly distributed, and opportunities are still not equally accessible among all people.

EDWIN: Don't you think it's a good idea to become a teacher so that I could make a difference in the lives of even a few children?

PHYLLIS: Yes, I agree! It's wonderful to make a difference in people's lives. However, it's not necessary to become a teacher in order to do that. You could become a foster parent, a coach, a rural doctor, a social worker, or a volunteer in a community center. You could open a shelter for homeless people, work for Habitat for Humanity, volunteer with the Boys and Girls Clubs, fight greed and corruption, and give food to hungry families. Any of those services would have more direct benefit to children's lives than teaching in schools, which have traditionally operated as socially reproductive institutions. In schools you can reach only a small segment of the population, and probably not the neediest people. Of those children who do attend, some are in school under duress because the law compels them to be there. If you want to make a difference in people's lives, there are more direct and effective ways to do that than becoming a teacher.

EDWIN: That's kind of depressing. It's just hard to accept that schooling has not been an effective way to help people improve their lives. At least as a teacher I'd be able to help children get along peaceably with other children, wouldn't I?

PHYLLIS: It sounds as though you want to become a teacher so you can help children develop virtues. Do you think that virtue can be taught?

EDWIN: Oh, now you're trying to trip me up with those dialogues in which Socrates argues with Meno, Protagoras, and Gorgias about whether virtue can be taught. Those are convoluted arguments, anyway. It always seemed to me that Plato was just trying to discredit the Sophists by any means necessary. Did you ever see a dialogue in which Socrates' opponent won, or in which Socrates changed his mind?

PHYLLIS: That's a good point. I guess it's kind of misleading to call those Platonic writings "dialogues."

EDWIN: Yes. The term "Socratic Dialogue" is a misnomer. They're really one-sided persuasive essays—you might even say rhetorical. But let's get back to the virtue thing. As a teacher, I could help students become better people—more compassionate, civic minded, and thoughtful. Don't you agree?

PHYLLIS: I can see what you're saying, but the teaching of virtue is difficult for several reasons. First, how are you going to know whether a particular act is virtuous or self-serving? Second, nobody can agree whether virtue should be measured by actions, intentions, or effects. Third, being knowledgeable about virtue is not the same as being virtuous. How can education change people from being non-virtuous to being virtuous? Finally, virtue is not the same across different cultures. Actions that are honorable in one culture may be immoral in another culture. Whose virtues are you going to promote in a diverse classroom?

EDWIN: Okay, I can see that cultivating virtue is not a compelling reason to become a teacher. But I have a better reason! In my classroom, the students will all have a voice in running the class because I will never be authoritarian. In my classroom, everyone will experience what democracy is supposed to feel like, and from our classroom experiences, students will develop the democratic skills and dispositions that they can take with them into the world.

PHYLLIS: How are you going to accomplish that? I mean how are you going to create a democratic classroom when the students in your class will be expecting a conventional classroom?

EDWIN: Well, doesn't everybody treasure freedom? Don't students want to be in a democratic environment where they can have a voice in the curriculum and be empowered to help run the class?

PHYLLIS: That has not been my experience.

EDWIN: What do you mean?

PHYLLIS: Well, a couple things. First, people don't always welcome change, especially in schools. Many people think democracy is not appropriate for classrooms anyway because it's not realistic; experience with participatory democracy in a classroom is not the most efficient way to prepare students to face the challenges of real life. Second, whenever I invite students to help construct the curriculum, they accuse me of not doing my job. They say, "We are the students and you are the teacher. Our taxes pay you to fulfill certain responsibilities, and we need your expertise in order to succeed."

EDWIN: I guess they have a point. The teacher is responsible for helping students get the required curriculum. That's what teachers are held accountable for.

PHYLLIS: But those are not the only problems. Democracy is hard. People have to be well informed about issues, they have to have good communication skills, and they have to be open minded to many contradictory viewpoints. With the knowledge, skills, and dispositions that are necessary in order for democracy to work, it's extraordinarily difficult to establish democratic environments. Democracy in a classroom is even harder to enact when the rest of the school is organized in the usual way with hierarchies of administration in which students are expected to follow directions and respect authority.

EDWIN: Well, as a teacher, I would be able to teach the skills that are necessary for democratic participation, wouldn't I?

PHYLLIS: I totally support those goals. But there's another problem. To be democratic means that everybody gets to have a voice in how the school is run. What do you think most people want from school?

EDWIN: I suppose different people want different things, but primarily, people want schools to give them the tools necessary to lead successful and productive lives.

PHYLLIS: I agree. And that means most parents want their children to have the experiences, skills, and credentials that traditional authoritarian schools provide. For the most part, people want schools to help them get ahead in the world.

EDWIN: But democracy is the most important thing for people to learn in school! Shouldn't that take priority?

PHYLLIS: For the majority of families, the main purpose of school should be to prepare people to lead productive lives. If you think the most important purpose of school is to rehearse democracy, then you're in the minority. How can it be a democracy if most people are voting against it? Do you want to impose democracy by forcing a cultural revolution? That would be a little ironic, don't you think?

EDWIN: But you can't be saying that teaching is totally a waste of time, can you?

PHYLLIS: I'm not saying that at all. It also depends on what you think teaching means, and how teaching is related to learning.

EDWIN: What do you mean?

PHYLLIS: Well, students do not learn everything that teachers intend for them to learn, and conversely, students learn things in school that teachers do not intend for them to learn.

EDWIN: Sure, people in school learn all the implicit or "hidden" curriculum stuff— how to sit still, how to stand in line, how to fake attention when you're bored, and when to keep your mouth shut so you don't get in trouble.

PHYLLIS: You have a good understanding of curriculum theories!

EDWIN: Plus, learning depends on the student, not only on the teacher. If people are going to get educated, they have to be actively engaged; they have to take ownership of their own learning.

PHYLLIS: In that case, how can you separate the effects of a teacher's teaching from the effects of a student's studying? Getting a good education depends on many things besides the teacher, so it's virtually impossible to verify any cause-and-effect relationship between teaching and learning.

EDWIN: I suppose that's true. But sometimes people can learn by example. Isn't that how we begin learning when we are children?

PHYLLIS: Yes, I agree there is considerable evidence that people learn by example— for better or worse.

EDWIN: So it seems I would be able teach democratic citizenship by leading an exemplary life.

PHYLLIS: If that's true, then what's the difference between being a teacher and being a regular person?

EDWIN: You're so cynical! It seems you're saying there are no good reasons to become a teacher. But if nobody becomes a teacher, then what will happen to society? How will children have any chance to succeed in the world?

PHYLLIS: There are also no good reasons to climb mountains, compose symphonies, or write poems. Can you point to any evidence that teachers have made the world into a place that is safer, more equitable, or more beautiful?

EDWIN: What are you talking about?! What would count as evidence for such a claim? Do you mean to say that it's a bad idea to become a teacher?

PHYLLIS: I am not saying that it's bad, only that it is dangerous.

EDWIN: What do you mean by "dangerous"?

PHYLLIS: The danger is that teachers sometimes have to choose between safeguarding the collective good and preventing harm to any individual.

EDWIN: That's an ethical problem that no political or economic theory has ever solved! Now who's the idealist?!

PHYLLIS: Oh. I guess you're right.

EDWIN: So what do you mean by "harm," anyway?

PHYLLIS: As far as teaching is concerned, I'm particularly concerned about one common harmful practice that's usually justified in the name of the collective good, namely punishment.

EDWIN: You can't be serious! Punishment isn't ideal, but there's no other way to manage a classroom. What about logical consequences? Get real!

PHYLLIS: Fair enough. Logical consequences are one thing, and they are not necessarily harmful. But classroom consequences are not always logical; they're often legalistic or normative. Sometimes those consequences include an element of punishment, and that's a problem.

EDWIN: But punishment is very effective for getting results! Besides, almost everybody does it.

PHYLLIS: I agree that punishment is very effective for getting results; so are tasers and psyops. But ethically speaking, punishment is harmful; and instrumentally speaking, punishment makes people learn the wrong things. Punishment is effective for making people learn how to feel bad about themselves and to develop attitudes of resentment and alienation. Moreover, good people who punish others also feel bad about themselves for having harmed another person. Just because many people use punishment doesn't make it okay.

EDWIN: How else are you going to teach students to do the right thing?!

PHYLLIS: Well, that's what all those learning theories are for—to give teachers a range of alternative possibilities to choose from. Even behaviorism rejects punishment in favor of reinforcements! But there are many learning theories besides behaviorism including cognitivism, constructivism, humanism, critical pedagogy, invitational, facilitative, problem-based, discovery, and a bunch more.

EDWIN: How can teachers decide which learning theories to use?

PHYLLIS: For me, that's a question of ethics. The first step is to agree that punishment is ethically unacceptable. Then from there, it becomes possible to think through other alternatives.

EDWIN: This is getting complicated. How can teachers figure out what is ethical?

PHYLLIS: That's what philosophy and educational theories are for. "Ethical" can mean many different things.

EDWIN: Okay. What does "ethical" mean to you?

PHYLLIS: For me, personally, "ethical" has two parts, both of which are dynamic:

- Keep challenging my assumptions about what is good.
- Do less harm next time.

EDWIN: Wow, you sound totally pessimistic, even nihilistic!

PHYLLIS: I may be pessimistic, but I'm not nihilistic. After all, I've been a teacher for almost 30 years. I'm just saying that before anyone decides to take up our profession, it's important to know that as a teacher, it is easier to do more harm than good. There are always unintended consequences to our actions, and the stakes are exceedingly high because we have other people's lives in our care.

EDWIN: Then why are you a teacher?

PHYLLIS: That's a good question. Teaching is the most fascinating phenomenon I've ever encountered, and I guess being a teacher allows me to study teaching from the inside. Teaching is mostly hard work, but I love it.

EDWIN: Do you mean because it's so rewarding when you see people learn and succeed?

PHYLLIS: No, I don't mean that. I mean that good teaching is gratifying in and of itself. Of course, it's always delightful to watch people discover and create, but that's a separate issue.

EDWIN: So you're talking about the experience of teaching as an intrinsic value, not as an instrumental means to some end?

PHYLLIS: Yes, exactly. The crucial thing, though, is not why we become teachers in the first place, but what kind of teachers we become.

EDWIN: Absolutely. If I'm going to become a teacher, I want to become a good teacher.

PHYLLIS: That's the whole point, and the most vexing point because "good teacher" is almost impossible to define.

EDWIN: What do you mean?

PHYLLIS: Well, because different people value such different things: from warm caring relationships, to improvement of test scores, to effective management skills. For me, "What is a good teacher?" has been a life-long question and the reason I care so much about educational theories. I had always hoped that my life as a teacher could bring more peace and justice into the world, but along the way I have found that every path is strewn with boobytraps.

EDWIN: Because when we act with knowledge, care, and the best of intentions, things can still go wrong, and people can still get hurt.

PHYLLIS: Yes, that's it exactly. And that's why good teachers always think so long and hard about their words and actions.

EDWIN: What do you live by when you think about being a "good teacher"?

PHYLLIS: At the moment, my main thing is "Do less harm next time."

EDWIN: I still don't know if I'll go into teaching, but now I have a better grasp of how compelling the challenges are. I guess I'll have to think very carefully about that.

PHYLLIS: Thank you. We need more people with brilliant minds, kind hearts, and generous spirits to become teachers. Whatever you decide, I hope you'll always respect teaching as a vital responsibility and a humbling honor.

Philosophy of Education is Bent

Cris Mayo

Published online: 24 April 2011
© Springer Science+Business Media B.V. 2011

Abstract Troubled times in education means that philosophers of education, who seem to never stop making defenses of our field, have to do so with more flexibility and a greater understanding of how peripheral we may have become. The only thing worse than a defensive philosopher is a confident and certain philosopher, so it may be that our very marginality will give us renewed energies for problematizing education. Occupying our marginal position carefully and in concert with other marginal inquiries, I think, will do our field good. Because of its attention to what it takes to be willing to learn and to approach theoretical and real world obstacles with open if cautious interest, philosophy of education is about holding concepts and movements in tension, bending the implications of commonplace, commonsensical ideas about education, and carefully examining the all of these maneuvers for the exclusions they wittingly and unwittingly produce. Problematizing the certainties derived from majoritarian positions, be it whiteness, Westernness, or any other dominant perspective, can provide us with a diversity of claims to scrutinize and epistemological positions to be wary of.

Keywords Philosophy of education · Accountability · Queer · Marginality

In a political context where colleges of education come under fire for their attention to peripheral topics like "democracy and education" when, according to critics, they should be more interested in accountability, those of us in social foundations of education and philosophy of education now find ourselves trying to conserve the radicalism of past critiques of education in the face of new right attempts to expunge not only the radical intervention of so-called "identity politics" but the "classics" like Dewey and Plato. These are hard times, like other times. It seems like every generation of philosophers of education run up against some kind of hard time or other that encourages us to assert the need to stop and think, to be aware of the structuring tensions of education, and to also push for hopeful

C. Mayo (✉)
Department of Education Policy, Organization and Leadership and Department of
Gender and Women's Studies, University of Illinois at Urbana-Champaign,
1310 S. Sixth St., Champaign, IL 61820, USA
e-mail: cmayo@illinois.edu

responses to those tensions. Yet now as the definition of education seems to be set by local governments and school supervisors who think mass firings will solve all the problems caused by underfunding and accountability, there are moments, too, of unexpected transnational hospitality and common cause, examples of difference finding connection. At the same time the mayor of Providence, Rhode Island decides to fire all the teachers to give himself the budgetary flexibility he needs, protestors in Egypt send dozens of pizzas to support demonstrators in Madison, Wisconsin who are trying to protect the collective bargaining rights of public employees, teachers included. Protest signs in Wisconsin urge the public to "Walk Like an Egyptian" and join mass protests to reinvigorate democracy, just like our northern African counterparts are doing—a parallel nearly unthinkable and even more remarkable when the Egyptians are modeling democracy for a US state with a long, vibrant labor history. In a context where innovations that would race us to the top while undermining the labor that might get us there, philosophers of education, more interested in critical engagement than definite outcomes, may look all the more out of step and disconnected. But I think we are also conservationists, pushing those in educational institutions to resituate their activities in enduring questions about knowledge, ethics, and progressive educational movements.

We are also facing a sense of ourselves as conservative on a related front. Educational institutions seem less interested in what we take to be the deeper and more complicated questions that define education and are increasingly more interested in science-based measurements that only measure a thin range of what learning might mean (largely because that's all that can be measured). In higher education, also driven by new financial pressures and the same ideological and economic interests that have shifted public education, the humanities are passé. Whether works are from ancient Greece, the Harlem Renaissance or contemporary feminist and queer political theory, they are increasingly viewed as all of a piece. Now more than ever, thinking about how to build democratic societies that respect diversity and difference is crucial, not only to critique the kinds of educational reforms that are turning learning into test taking but also to reassert how the humanities and engagement with others enables political and educational development. For philosophers of education, this means rethinking or at least more strongly articulating why we critiqued the canon but also coming to the defense of canonical studies that are as under fire for irrelevancy or lack of certain financial benefit. This means bringing together what had seemed to be the study at the center of the world, philosophy, and the studies of those on the margins. Over the last few decades in philosophy of education I think there has been quite a bit of grumbling on either side of that divide—either philosophers are all elitists who don't examine the implicit racism and sexism of their approaches or feminists and people of color are destroying the rigor of philosophical work. At this point, we're all in the same sort of trouble and need to be thinking and working together, even if we disagree. We may need to return to some points of contention during the canon wars and rethink how to bridge some of our disciplinary differences in the humanities and perhaps more fully understand—as some suggested at the time—that our methods of inquiry are quite similar, with similar aims. Though our textual choices may be different and yes, we may have distinctly different epistemological starting points, we at least have in common our relative remove from the new technocracies. I think what those of us still committed to broadening the canon might bring to such a discussion is perhaps a repetition of our earlier points as well: methods of critical thinking and learning that canonical texts in the humanities engender points not only to forms of citizenship and thinking but also to a rationale for expanding beyond traditional disciplinary studies. But our colleagues can also say back to us: yes, and part of the way you learned all that was through the criticality and forms of reading made possible by texts millennia in age.

Whatever different texts and traditions we work from, philosophy of education is increasingly seen as either irrelevant or disparaged. As education races to the top of science-driven research and programs to improve outcomes to forms of education that seem to have spawned administrative cheating on tests and dissolution of teachers unions, our attention to the ends and means of education seems to miss the point, seems to queer the project of accountability. Maybe those with a longer view can see this has happened before with teacher-proof curricula, some other technocratic ascendency, or critique of the humanities. Maybe these aren't the only times of crisis in the field but this crisis and the claim that higher education will never be the same again, means that philosophers of education, who seem to never stop making defenses of our field, have to do so with more flexibility and a greater understanding of how peripheral we may have become. The only thing worse than a defensive philosopher is a confident and certain philosopher, so it may be that our very marginality will give us renewed energies for problematizing education. Occupying our marginal position carefully and in concert with other marginal inquiries, I think, will do our field good.

Knowing that we need to assert our diverse presence clearly does not mean that we answer this new educational industry in ways its machinery can easily understand. In times that demand easy answers that have been destructive, philosophy of education, I think, needs to maintain its problem-posing approach and encourage students to think through the dangers caused by certainty but to also maintain a curiosity about how to approach these problems. Because of its attention to what it takes to be willing to learn and to approach theoretical and real world obstacles with open if cautious interest, philosophy of education is about holding concepts and movements in tension, bending the implications of commonplace, commonsensical ideas about education, and carefully examining the all of these maneuvers for the exclusions they wittingly and unwittingly produce. Problematizing the certainties derived from majoritarian positions, be it whiteness, Westernness, or any other dominant perspective, can provide us with a diversity of claims to scrutinize and epistemological positions to be wary of.

How do philosophies and practices of education encourage learners to have the confidence to name their concerns and identities without falling into certainties that cannot be disrupted by further critical engagement? To get to some of these issues I have been interested in forms of communication and subjectivity that seem to have inbuilt appreciation for complex communication. Rather than relying on certainty and directness, they have a tactical understanding that one not only may not say all one means to say in the interests of civility but that still try to maintain and complicate connections across differences. The forms of indirect communication and partial understandings that derive from interactions across differences may be helpful reminders that everything does not need to be clear and measurable in order to have a positive effect. Because as close as we may get to one another, we may not come to easy understandings or even enduring concord but at least we're trying. Philosophy of education, with its attention to the difficulties of knowing and ethics, may help us to understand that even if that we cannot get to central problems of living together and thinking together in a context of difference because things are not resolvable nonetheless we can continue to uneasily approach these challenges sideways. Bending the time and meaning of discussions itself stops, however momentarily, the machinery of educational institutions and easy superiorities.

Educational philosophy, I hope, gives students pause enough to think about openness to innovation and challenge and also yet gives us a sense of why it would be important to stay committed to at least some, however open and indeterminate sense of justice. I recently heard myself described as a philosopher of education who wants everyone to be a lesbian. It seemed an odd description at first but as I think about what philosophy of education can do to encourage people engage in blatant forms of critique, and to make them sensitive to the kinds of disapproval that those critical acts may engender, especially in these times of tighter budgets and irrational accountabilities. When funds that would have been used to improve public schools are now allocated to smaller charter and other schools that will not necessarily even need to indicate an interest in serving the public good, and when in the US colleges of education are encouraged to make common cause with political forces trying to disempower teachers unions, I think it is becoming clearer that careful philosophical engagement with foundational issues in education are seeming queerer and queerer. As programs that centralize philosophy of education, too, are becoming fewer and far between, it may appear that philosophy of education has been broken by the new ac-countabilities. I'm hoping for the sake of education as an actual undertaking as opposed to an industry that philosophy of education is just bent, it isn't yet broken.

While I don't want to overuse queer or turn it into just another form of critical ratio-nality, queering education and doing the kind of philosophy of education that is cheerfully queer may entail turning to tentative judgments and sideways forms of thinking and speaking, trying to use puzzles of invitation and challenge to get at difficulties of under-standing among people, thinking through the problems associated with teaching and learning, and thinking more about the institutional structures that are turning energetic education into routines of testing and measurement. Philosophy of education is hospitable in its attempts to sort out diverse and divergent commitments and challenging in its unwillingness to let any aspect of those commitments go without critique and intervention. Queer interventions seem a way into these sorts of strategies for engagement: queerness is both a way of looking at the normative world sideways and has historically deployed subtle forms of communication and knowing that operate out of intuition, rage, and affection. Queerness, like other forms of critical knowledge, draws on desire, speculation, and even blatant, spectacular curiosity. Because everyone lives under normative systems to which they cannot possibly conform, the ability to be queer and to engage in acts queering concepts and practices, I think, extends to everyone. Although the kind of philosophy of education that emerges from queer experiences may undertake these strategies of dis-cerning, yearning for, and disrupting as almost second nature, they are also strategies that most people have some ability to engage, especially from the margins. And clearly phi-losophy of education is being pushed to the margins of educational discourse. Indeed, the trickiest thing in these days where education is becoming more and more normatively framed as accountability, is to stimulate criticality. It may well be that give the very strong turn to education-science and evidenced-based education, philosophers of education cannot easily find discursive traction to mount a head-on critique of this institutional shift and now have to find more sideways and bent tactics.

At the risk of pushing the queer metaphor too far, philosophy of education is increas-ingly described as elite (rich over educated people with who don't have to teach children), debauched (we spend too much time thinking and don't plan for Mondays), and perverse in our attachment to obscure and rarefied things (like those odd antique store owners)–and maybe, oddly, not promiscuous enough in our attempts to make the educational philosophy seem more appealing to more people. We do need to recruit, building on the latent forms of critique that go with any connection to education and making more of a spectacle of philosophy as a form of thinking and acting that is not interested in reproduction of norms. I think that queering philosophy of education means that we can think about futurity—our own as well as more generally– without being tied to the increasingly stringent and purportedly "practical" concerns that are so damaging to education's potential.

The tasks I take to be central are encouraging time out from the normal routine, taking a bent perspective on reading and acting, and recruiting others. Time out has probably always been a challenge but now that our students are working more hours than ever to support themselves through school or returning to graduate school. They do this while working full time or attending classes online in time zones that don't match well for synchronous sessions, that time apart from routine becomes more difficult to access. Ubiquitous learning may be encouraging us to see micro-forms of time apart, squeezing in contemplation between waiting for the bus and jostling for a seat. Time to think, let alone time to read and time to communicate with others about reading and thinking, seems a luxury. Trying to encourage students and colleagues to make time when there simply isn't time is a daunting task. Refiguring the times we have together into something like stolen moments for deep thinking becomes all the more important. But attempts to take time or make time also punctuated by students who do want to know what this thinking has to do with them and what it will do for them specifically on Monday (a phrase I would like to outlaw but one that I also recognize is an indication that there is no time for luxuries like thinking and only time for acting, these are the pressures we all work under in a system of accountability that does not account for education but rather replaces it).

As irritating as it may be to shift the meaning of key concepts in education as students and teachers of philosophy of education, redefining the time of education gives us a place to start. Shaking students out of their habitual relationship to action means interrupting them, literally stopping the time of activity to make it an object of scrutiny. Interrupting people is always an affront, a confrontation that demands attention where there had been none and that entails a refocusing from whatever the background to one's habits is to the sudden appearance of another. Interrupting normal time is I think always startling, irritating, and after a while, when students have been in school for a long time or our colleagues are trying to get on with what they are accustomed to doing, also a sort of boring interruption too. Thinking that does not produce an immediately identifiable and quantifiable product is wasteful in a context that is structured to only understand bottom lines. So our interruptions are not only irritating and boring, they are unproductive, the sort of excess that needs to be cut in order for responsible thinking and acting to take place. To return to queerness, though, excess in the midst of normal time is meant to be a disruptive spectacle that in turn shows the problems in time and practice as usual, literally how much time is spent avoiding thinking about the pressures of time and the requirement of quiet time or time talking together. For teachers, this is not a remarkable problem—their own experiences with having professional development periods and free periods cut in order to make education more efficient easily shows them the value of such time. Increasingly, this time apart is harder to find and harder to justify because it does not fit with the reproductive norms of education.

In education, where so many students don't want to talk in class because "that's so gay," it is hard to be nonconforming and passionately involved with studies or ideas. So the desire to learn is itself is queer. It's remarkable that wanting to learn is marked out as something odd enough to comment upon. It isn't normal to have passion for one's studies. Still, for all the weariness we may experience when trying to teach students who are themselves weary at the pressures that will be put on them as teachers to produce, not inspire, our students do enjoy—despite their initial protestations– the intimacy of intellectual connection and the intensity of learning, debate, and classroom discussion. Discussion, after all, is where they appear, make themselves anew through engagement with new ideas. Even in times where education appears stultifying in so many places, students remake themselves through ideas and interchange, they also identify with and as identities that they may or may not wind up being. And that also makes the scene of education a very queer place.

There are imaginative possibilities that arise in the process of learning together and that shift people, challenging who they were and moving them into places and ideas they hadn't anticipated. These dynamics are happening in every energetic class and may even happen in classes that don't intend to generate that kind of energy. And sometimes the process of rethinking and remaking relationships can create anxieties. Coming at this task obliquely, inciting rethinking rather than demanding it, suggesting new possibilities for education and encouraging critical engagement, rather than setting out clear plans, in short, setting out the dilemmas and puzzles of education and trying to work them out together are, I think, the tasks of philosophers of education. Part of an engaged philosophy of education may involve coming to students and issues where they are, shifting in a more mobile form of philosophy of education that engages in conversations with stakeholders who are working through problems in education.

From the older tradition of Socrates wandering around Athens and getting waylaid by people with whom he disagreed, philosophers of education can also, with the approval of the district, school, institutional review board or whoever, take our projects to schools and talk with people, bringing philosophical tools to bear on what have been ethnographic and qualitative research's purview. While philosophy has prided itself on having questions and answers that endure beyond particular contexts, particular contexts themselves can bring out new ways of thinking. So it may be that focusing on the subtleties of intersubjective communication and not only philosophizing but doing research with actual subjects is a way for us to take philosophy of education back to where people are making diverse meanings out of their education and to find out what they're doing and how they're communicating with one another. By finding more spaces in which to do philosophy of education with others, including engaging these questions with people in public schools, we can help to underscore how people are critical, despite policies intent on having them be otherwise. This means making more of a spectacle out of the process of philosophizing about education, marking the time for thinking as ubiquitous but also distinctly bent.

Philosophy of Education in a Poor Historical Moment: A Personal Account

Ilan Gur-Ze'ev

Published online: 1 May 2011
© Springer Science+Business Media B.V. 2011

Abstract   Under the post-metaphysical sky "old" humanistic-oriented education is possible solely at the cost of its transformation into its negative, into a power that is determined to diminish human potentials for self-exaltation. Nothing less than total
metamorphosis is needed to rescue the core of humanistic genesis: the quest for edifying
Life and resistance to the call for "home-returning" into the total harmony that is promised
to us within nothingness.

Keywords   Humanism · New progressive thinking · Old progressive thinking · Diasporic
philosophy · Transcendence · Self-annihilation of the West

It was in an unusually rainy day in February 1955 when I was born to the Vilcek family in
Haifa. From my present perspective I can recollect that "Haifa" did very little to become
genuinely humanist. It was obsessed much more with finding some respite from the har-
rowing insistent cries of mothers and fathers; parents of my friends who after they went to
bed at night began to let loose awful secrets about children, sisters, parents from "there"
who were killed in endless impossible ways; addressing immediate as well as two
millennia of accumulated memories, strives and worthy suffering that were suppressed or
sublimated. A special role was reserved here for the disguise through daily secular routines
of an ostensible normality within the framework of personal and national emancipation, or
at least, within the process of cultivating a new generation of Jews, *Sabars*, who would
grow up to become people capable of not losing their mind or their consciousness. The
highest of aims was to become partners in the edification of a worthy society that will
constitute a paragon, a light to all nations on earth. And so, from my early childhood, I was
faced with the responsibility of maturing into a master violinist or at least a very famous
writer. You could not compromise with my mother on anything less than that. The two
pillars of my education at that stage of my life were Ze'ev Jabotinsky's *Death—or con-
quering the mountain* on the one hand, and my father's *Never ever—but really—never ever*

I. Gur-Ze'ev (✉)
Haifa, Israel
e-mail: ilangz@edu.haifa.ac.il

give up! My father's mantra had a special tone for my young ears. After all, he was the only corpse in the Mauthausen concentration camp that recollected itself and came back to life from the mass grave into which it was thrown by the Nazis after his execution. Halisa, our neighborhood, was not just an arena of remembrance of the silenced presence of the Arab neighbors who in 1948, after losing the merciless battle they initiated, fled the city in terror and left behind dreams of a better future, old cooking pots, colorful ceramics and mourning houses. For us, the kids of Halisa, it was at the same time also the land of hugging sun, wonders and hope. Oh hope, Oh hope!

Nevertheless, Halisa was an emissary that devoted itself to the humanist promise that within an effective *purity* the conditions are set for the betterment of human qualities, the progress of knowledge, a personal as well as national psychic and epistemological balance and cultural flourishing—if only we could be genuinely creative and brave enough.

As a typical showground of modern Jewish national revival, Halisa was truly committed to educate for *courage*. Accordingly, at the age of three I already watched *Michael Strogoff* at *Vered*, the neighborhood cinema, as a pedagogical preparation for my manhood soon to come. In retrospect I can say that for our family viewing *Michael Strogoff* enabled a meeting between the resolute Omsk-born Russian hero and the decisiveness of Zionist education to give birth to "the new Jew" who would not go like sheep to the slaughter, would be unbelievably creative in the old-new homeland, and would defeat not only the Diaspora as a temporary-predatory home but also Diaspora as a Jewish ideal and universal mission. As a Zionist version of the humanist agenda this educational project carried a strong Universalist commitment. In its non-ethnocentric manner it was supposed to manifest the quest for returning "home" into harmony, symmetry and balance of the kind that calls us back "home" to nothingness, an invitation that totally negates the spirit and contents of Jewish Diasporic *Messianism without a Messiah*.

The *Vered* cinema was an arena for various and widely different family experiences. Some were very local. I can still hear the neighbors shouting, "Stop the screening and wait, the Vilceks are coming, the Vilceks are coming!" For our family a film such as *Michael Strogoff* must have been not merely a local experience. At least for my grandmother, my mother and my father it must also have been an occasion to revisit powerful memories, memories of East Europe and Russia, memories such as the ever green fields and endless ways in which their non-Jewish neighbors killed their relatives in the Slovac town of Levice only a minute before the Nazi army actually entered it. Or the memories of Keyla, my wonderful grandmother, who on April 6, 1903, at the age of 16 in the city of Kishinev saved her sisters and brothers from slaughter by their neighbors who came with sticks, kitchen knives and bare hands to kill Keyla and the entire family, as they did to so many other Jewish families in that particular pogrom. These memories were interwoven with fresh memories of the despair and bravery of our young men and women in Israel's War of Independence that had been fought only few years earlier. The historical, literary, and anti-Diasporic Jewish psychic representations culminated in an educational Eros that insisted on becoming a garden of Enlightenment in the wilderness. This powerful movement insisted on a humanist future in the old-new homeland, as against what they saw as the barbaric eastern reality into which they had arrived. In all its rich aspects that light of my childhood in Wadi Halisa in the 1950s has become impossible under the present post-metaphysical skies.

As an invitation to holy progress and transcendence, that humanist light has rather shamefully faded in a non-heroic and non-tragic manner. Presently it has no presence as the manifestation of Eros, as a call to give birth to strives or rebirth, as *hope* that was so vividly present in Halisa of the 1950s. The holiness of that vitality has been exiled, along with the preconditions for salvation by a humanist killing-God-each-moment-anew. Halisa has become an impossible possibility in the form of concrete utopian manifestations of naivety, courage, Eros and responsibility for justice or for great deeds such as the endeavors of Michael Strogoff, the heroes of Karl May or the heroic Israeli pioneers, who for the last 100 years despite the enmity of the governing power on the one hand and the violent reception by the local Arabs and Bedouins (who did not know that they were soon to become "Palestinians") on the other, insisted on working the high-cost deserted land, fighting dysentery, and offering their sons and daughters a humanistic-oriented education.

This has become unfeasible in face of the entry into the arenas of mega-speed in the era of the exile of holiness and the triumph of post-metaphysical ecstasy and postmodern spectacles; in the new factuality of hyper-reality there is no air for the breath of Utopia of a self-declared moral avant-garde, or for the promise of edifying humanity or for its deification within which it progresses toward responding to the invitation of Eros; an invitation that begins at the moment of Genesis of the destruction of nothingness, which is also the birth moment of the invitation to "home-returning" which during the history of the dialectics of immanence and transcendence has also given birth to so many offspring (who are Thanatos-oriented) adorned as the agents of Love of Life.

Under the post-metaphysical sky "old" humanistic-oriented education is possible solely at the cost of its transformation into its negative, into a power that is determined to diminish human potentials for self-exaltation. Nothing less than total metamorphosis is needed to rescue the core of humanistic genesis: the quest for edifying Life and resistance to the call for "home-returning" into the total harmony that is promised to us within nothingness.

As for me, in the last couple of years a new beginning has become a must; to save that which is worthy to be saved, to redeem that which is redeemable, to re-invent that which is to be transformed, and, most of all, to give birth to hope. But what are the still possible gateways for a humanist in a post-humanistic era? Could it be that it is morally wrong to offer a non-oppressive humanist education in an era that is devoted to the destruction of the preconditions for the edification of humanity, an historical moment at which relating to humanity as an agent for supreme transcendence is considered a unique version of violence that should be challenged by all possible means? In response to the question of humanistic-oriented education in a post-humanist era it is of relevance to say few words about the specific *togetherness* of Diasporic humans. I will address this togetherness by articulating some characteristics and potentials of the *Orcha*.

Orcha, the Hebrew word for a caravan of camels, commodities and humans in the desert, is a telos, a negative Utopia that is actualized in, or absent altogether from a concrete reality and is enabled solely for individuals. Never for collectives. In its essence Counter-education is dedicated to the affirmation of Life. As part of the *Orcha*, it is the grand affirmation of Diasporic life, an unreserved "Yes!" to eternal Love of Life; it is an enduring mature homeless-improvisational co-poiesis. Improvisation here goes hand in hand with responsibility; responsibility for enduring transcendence, responsibility for enduring self-positioning and becoming courageous and gay. Courageous gayness enables happiness when it becomes a holy work, an erotic co-poiesis which extends a hand to the otherness, even when it is the alterity of the other.

Diasporic counter-education is dedicated to the cultivation of seriousness, joyous seriousness, which gives birth to irony as against cynicism and mechanistic attitudes to courage. As such it maddens the (anti-humanistic-oriented) new progressivists. At the same time it is met with disregard by the rapidly growing mass of disciples of the quest to be totally swallowed by the postmodern pleasure machine. In the last couple of years I have found it impossible to continue what I have been doing as a matter of dogmatic routine quite easily in academia and public life for the last 20 years. I felt that I could not go on with the celebrated dogmatic-ecstatic cult of radical "critique" and fashionable leftist "resistance", even if participating in this new progressivist feast almost automatically ensures international academic status, high income, easygoing self-forgetfulness and endless invitations to the most prestigious academic arenas. It is so tempting and profitable to participate in this ecstatic bacchanalia first and foremost as a quasi-religious *purification* among the majority in the West; disciples of the new meta-narrative even when their consciousness and rhetoric are still loyal to "old" (humanist-oriented) progressivism, even if the organization of their psyche, their new openness and sensitivities are already part of the "new" progressivism. Many of these friends and colleagues are outraged by my present work.

Why does my new work irritate so many of the new progressivists in such strange and sometimes embarrassing ways? Is it because part of my attempt is to think about thinking that is beyond the modern-postmodern educational struggle? Or is it because of my insistence on paving paths to a religious erotic dynamic? Or is it because of the clash between responsibility to Life as against the struggle in the service of Thanatos and its call back "home" within two rival anti-Diasporic agents of the new progressive thinking: (1) a postmodern agenda with the support of anti-Enlightenment heroes such as Deleuze, Baudrillard, Karl Schmitt, Heidegger and Nietzsche and (2) an anti-postmodern new progressivism under the flags of Zizek, Badiou and Lenin. And where do these rival new-progressivists meet? Before the shrine where they ecstatically crucify "the Jew" again. Anti-Judaism (and anti-Judeo-Christian civilization) has become the gate to quasi-redemptive ecstasies in the absence of any redeeming authority.

Today education does not dwell in any particular locus. Education has become an open question. Facing its impossibility is one of its actualized forms of self-presentation. While normalizing education is always positioned in a specific arena, even in the form of mega-speed and hyper-reality arenas, counter-education is well aware of its aim to prepare us in a worthy manner for life in the *Orcha*, for the eroticism of eternal nomadism not solely within a specific "home" and its diverse borders but also and even much more so in-between, in the nowhere land between different space–time relations. As preparation for a worthy Diasporic existence within cracks and transgressions, Diasporic counter-education is the manifestation of *the totally other* to the "home-returning" call. It is an improvised, happy way of life that in the form of the *Orcha*, is always on the move, never hindering an improvised co-poiesis as a form of Love of Life.

Counter-education differs from normalizing education at once in its homeless genesis. The Odyssey of the *Orcha* has no end, not just no "home"; and yet it does have a challenge to address, and a never-complete essence to actualize. Counter-education is an eternal becoming-toward-the-world. It is never settled in one particular, or isolated, arena. It is a Utopian occurrence, a flow. Always under way. It is never solely "horizontal" nor is it solely "vertical", like a prayer in the monotheistic religions. Even when enclosed within a specific arena such as a post-modern, a modern or a pre-modern, it is never to be con-trolled, domesticated or reduced to an unproblematic reduction or formula.

Diasporic philosophy teaches us that every attempt to enlighten the "location" or even the paths of counter-education must bear in mind the rich effects and dynamic "mutual influences" within each arena, and among the various arenas, as against the illusions of dichotomous positioning such as "modern education", "democratic education", "feminist education", "spiritual education" and so forth. Normalizing education is enabled by its specificity within a concrete showground, determined by concrete preconditions, reactions of defined enemies, and other reactions and infiltrations which might be reconstructed and "properly" addressed. Counter-education is different in its preconditions, essence and aims. It is never the outlet or agent of a specific "home", never an agent of specific interests, agendas or origins beyond its Diasporic negative Utopia. The Diasporic human must challenge these and other manifestations of the given. He should prepare himself to crisscross arenas, cultural streams, different space–time relations and horizons of different kinds. Yet most of all, the religious Diasporic of the post-secular world must prepare himself and us for an existence within different "houses", "in-between" as well as in a "no-man's-land" that is dynamically located in the space between different arenas, unknown space–time relations, as well as unique or undeciphered and too familiar historical, bodily, moral and spiritual relations and contexts. Normalizing education will melt like snow in Sahara before such richness. But counter-education will be enhanced by such dangerous and enabling openness because it has a holy mission. Because it takes seriously its responsibility to continue the striving of Life for transcending improvisational co-poiesis as against the various, competing "home-returning" invitations to nothingness as our eternal "home".

Diasporic philosophy enables counter-education by its insistence that the human subject is some-one and not something, that there is much more in the subject than the contingent power relations within specific arenas. No human is thrown totally on the mercy of local and universal manipulations, nor is she an effect of the arbitrariness of the infinity of the moment. While the Diasporic human too is called back "home" into the consensus, harmony, total victory, truth or other agents of nothingness, she insists on Diasporic existence within the *Orcha*. This is her *Derech-Eretz*, her Diasporic existence-on-the-move. This is because for the Diasporic human both meaninglessness and determinism become *a gate to openness*, to self-elevation and rebirth within Diasporic togetherness; openness knocks on the door of the freedom of the Diasporic human and awakens her maturity toward Love of Life as a starting point for counter-education, for cultivation of worthy post-secular perspectives of the survivors, of those of us who have made a decision for responsible, improvised co-poiesis that overcomes all calls to be swallowed in any kind of collectivism, nihilism and all other versions of the "home-returning" project.

As a genuine fruit of worthy Diasporic existence counter-education is never at home. On no account is it domesticated; always active in its nomadic crisscrossing specific arenas, concrete material, psychic and symbolic conditions with their specific histories and realities. The Diasporic dimension of counter-education is dedicated to refusing the invitation to enter a deep sleep as the too-long-awaited genuine Messiah. Diasporic existence is enabled within this dynamic multifariousness only in light of hope. Yet even attunement to hope is to be cultivated and is never a given fact. It is never self-evident, nor is it given cheap, in keeping with its nature to appear at an unexpected moment, or to refuse to burst in altogether.

The openness of broken Being is the Burning Bush that calls humans as they might become, yet are not-yet. Always, not-yet. The human never dwells alone on a remote island, away from her smoldering, but actualizes her blaze by her very existence in the sense of what she is and in the sense of her becoming-toward-the-world. As such, and only as such, the Diasporic human is an absent presence, a never-completed-stream, an infinity that every moment anew is called back "home" to nothingness while her responsibility to Life calls her to continue the act of creation, to join eternal improvised-mature co-poiesis. This is why the human is never the mere sum of her subjectification manipulations and is never to be reduced to a meaningless construct, not even to a mere victim of the deceiving power that is enabled by the blend and mutual relations of the different fields of time–space relations, speeds, symbolic exchange, material dynamics and the other games which call the human to accept self-forgetfulness and the forgetfulness of her forgetfulness, enabling the normalized human a deep sleep as a substitute for Diasporic existence.

Today's new progressivism offers self-forgetfulness under the flag of "nomadism" and "resistance" as a camouflage to deep sleep and self-forgetfulness. This is why *today education as an open question must be re-articulated*. And where is it being presently reformulated as the most enigmatic call? Under a Western post-metaphysical sky in face of the quest of Judeo-Christian civilization for self-annihilation. Our generation is unique. It is a generation that within Judeo-Christian civilization has exiled the killer-of-God-each-moment-anew, deconstructed and secular holiness, has taken the fragmented remains that have become estranged to their essence—even as bad memories—and disseminated them within the centrifugality of the various mega-speed hyper-realities. Holiness has been forced to flee and find refuge within the ecstatic meaninglessness of the postmodern pleasure machine at the cost of its transformation into its negative. Anti-Judaic commitment (as distinct from anti-Semitism) becomes the meta-narrative of a new kind of progressivism. This is the source of the vitality of post-humanistic progressivism, which while it calls for an alternative to the oppressive legacy of Judeo-Christian civilization opens the way to a new, unrestrained, violence. Sometimes under the flag of the unrestrained justification of the counter-violence of the victims and sometimes in light of the suggestive power of the idea of violence for the sake of an aimless violence, anti-Enlightenment is becoming stronger by the day.

The meaninglessness in a post-metaphysical era which exiled the killer of God must compensate itself for the loss of holiness. And it compensates itself with ever more ecstatic quasi-nomadism and openness to violence on the one hand, and to the invitation of the postmodern pleasure-machine on the other. Those of us with more attuned ears will however, hear another music also, the music of *the totally other*. This old-new music re-invites us to Love of Life. This is the moment of birth of counter-education from the womb of Diasporic existence.

Diasporic philosophy is a way-of-life, a flow of *Derech-Eretz* with infinite faces and a dynamics that cultivates existence within the *Orcha*. Within counter-education it prepares us for crisscrossing the different arenas, logics and powers and realizing Love of Life "in-between". At the same time it is also a flow of connecting the infinite differences of totality, and challenges the quest of its particles to accept the invitation to "home-returning" into nothingness. Its nomadic and its integrative dimensions alike fertilize improvised counter-education.

Diasporic counter-education is erotic in its essence: Love of Life enables transcendence within and in-between its endless arenas and dynamics as an alternative to the invitation of the world of Jihad, new progressivism and the pleasure machine, that are nothing but present-day manifestations of the quest for returning to nothingness. The eternal improviser flourishes within the *Orcha*. There response-ability is cultivated to respond-abilities of the kind that will be presented by *Derech-Eretz*. The Diasporic human accepts responsibility to Life as transcendence over a fragmented and self-negating cosmos, toward self-elevation-within-alterity, toward improvisation as the complementary dimension of joyous Love of Life. Counter-education addresses and cultivates the intimate connection between responsible improvisation and holiness, between commitment and irony and negative Utopia. It acknowledges that in the postmodern condition holiness is exiled and that gone are the preconditions for the edification of humanity in theocentric as well as homocentric *Zeitgeist*s. It acknowledges, however, that this also is a gate. A gate to holiness that is true to itself. Counter-education acknowledges that under the post-metaphysical sky Diasporic projects as well as "home-returning" projects are no longer actualized within a positive Utopia. This awareness is a first step to a non-naïve addressing of holiness in a post-secular era. Holiness becomes (in a negative manner) broken yet simple, as in the days of pre-agricultural civilizations when humans were at the beginning of cultivating their humanity, ate uncooked food, and there was still no established difference between prayer, singing and an improvised nomadic holy dance of existence. The mature eternal improviser is a consistent (negative) utopist. The realization of this negative utopianism is an improvisation enabled in the eternity of the moment, within specific material and symbolic conditions. Counter-education paves the way to coexistence between the flow of the eternal improviser, negative Utopia in action and the uniqueness of the holy co-poiesis within the *Orcha*.

The Diasporic dimensions of the *Orcha* do not run fast for negativism, deconstruction, nihilism or cynicism: it is committed to the holy work of Diasporic improvisation and transcendence; creation that begins with training in response-ability to improvisation and courage. The courage to hope and the power of ironic belief within Love of Life is the improvisation of the Diasporic human, her "home".

While the *Orcha* has no last, appeasing, station or nirvana, it does have an aim: the transcending realization of a non-Thanatos-oriented co-poiesis and not solely within the cosmos. Counter-education is a creative addressing of specific challenges within a concrete field; however, at the same time it also teaches to address the holiness of the clashes, integrations and a-sympathies between the countless particles and manifestations of infinity. Negative intimacy with the cosmos unites the different Diasporic individuals who meet in the *Orcha*. In the improvised responsible co-poieses men and women are invited, again, to experience intimacy with the cosmos within and in-between the infinity of the moment and the realities of the changing historical and existential actualities.

There are endless paths and gates to approach Diasporic counter-education. Among them we should mention cultivating responsible improvisation, rehearsing courage, training in mature self-love or healthy breathing in face of the violence of the new progressivism and its *Zeitgeist* in the era of the exile of Spirit. Diasporic philosophy shows us that not only counter-education is possible: possible even today are also philosophy of education and counter-education as holy work. Such a counter-education offers us gratitude and courage, meaning and *hope*. Hope that is not determined by or an agent of "success", "victory" or dogmatic radicalism which invite us all back "home" into nothingness as our total redemption. It is Diasporic hope, a non-optimistic hope that enables counter-education within the *Orcha*, the flourishing of Love of Life, and improvisational responsibility under the post-metaphysical sky.

What I Talk About When I Talk About Teaching and Learning

Carl Anders Säfström

Published online: 20 April 2011
© Springer Science+Business Media B.V. 2011

Abstract   In this text I discuss two events in which I learned something important about life and about education in order to formulate in a precise manner two propositions for my pedagogical creed. In focus for both are the interrelatedness of theory and life. The stories are told through the lenses of Emmanuel Levinas's and Jacques Rancière's thinking, but the stories also are shown to be essential in my understanding of their thinking. The first story is about learning ethics as a consequence of meeting an old man on a remote island and the second story is about teaching, when a young girl in a situation of war taught me something important about political life. In a final section I discuss briefly what those theoretical/practical experiences and memories bring to my understanding of education.

Keywords   Stories · Teaching · Learning · Theory · Life · Pedagogical creed

In this text I discuss two events in which I learned something important about life and about education. I tell these stories today in relation to other tools for understanding what happened than the ones I had then, and from a position of already being changed by these experiences. My inspiration for interpretation of the stories comes especially from Emmanuel Levinas and Jacques Rancière. Yet, I also hope to show how my understanding of Levinas and Rancière comes from those narratives. In connection to this, the text is about the relation between theory and life and how to make sense of its interrelatedness. I am not though claiming a symmetrical relation between these thinkers inspiring interpretations of different events making up a story. Telling a story like living a life is fundamentally not a symmetrical experience. So my pedagogical creed is held together by my asymmetrical stories, rather than by a symmetrical relation between the thinkers I refer to. The stories are not told sequentially, where one developmentally leads to the other; instead I see them as being "connected through the middle", as Donna Haraway said during a performance in Stockholm a couple of years ago. I'm inspired by her conviction about the importance of storytelling as not being

C. A. Säfström (✉)
School of Education, Culture and Communication, Mälardalen University,
Box 325, 631 05 Eskilstuna, Sweden
e-mail: carl.anders.safstrom@mdh.se

G. J. J. Biesta (ed.), *Making Sense of Education*, DOI: 10.1007/978-94-007-4017-4_9,   57
© Springer Science+Business Media Dordrecht 2012

organised around cause–and–effect logic. Rather the story unfolds itself as if it has its own life out of reach even for the storyteller and hooks up with other stories in multiple layers. Such is the nature of a story. Even so I want to use the two stories I relate here in order to try to formulate what is most important in education as a form of life. I will be talking about learning and teaching. And following Rancière, storytelling is just one of the things we actually can do when we claim to use our intelligence—the other is guessing.

First Story: About Learning

I was in my twenties, full of energy. I was, like all other male Swedes at that age, enrolled for obligatory military service. A military service that I refused to take part in as a soldier, since I did not wanted to become the only really dangerous part of a gun. I therefore did my service in the Red Cross instead. Anyhow, being enrolled by the military entitled you to extremely cheap train tickets for travelling in Sweden during your free time. I decided to take a trip to Fårö, which is a small island in the Baltic Sea just north of the island Gotland. Fårö (in English, "Scheep island") is mostly known to be the island where the film director Ingemar Bergman lived. Which really isn't that important in comparison to the mysterious beauty of the island, not least its light and spectacular beaches and stone formations and strangely composed forests, to say nothing of the wind and the sea. During this time the island felt like it was out of sync with the rest of the world. The bus picking me up at the harbour was an authentic 1954 Scania bus. Somehow it felt perfectly normal taking a bus ride in a time before my birth. The bus took me to a guesthouse where I intended to stay for a couple of days, while exploring the island. Biking the island was extremely popular in the early eighties, ever since a famous Swedish writer included it in a must-read novel. It was part of what one as an adventurous youngster should do (even though most of them stayed safe around Visby, the main capital of Gotland, smoking pot and drinking too many cheap beers). At the guesthouse by the sea I asked the owner of the house if there was possibly someone renting out bikes. He told me that there was an old man at the crossroad not too far from where we were. Full of enthusiasm for the day to come, I packed some things and went to rent myself a bike. It was a 30 min' walk before I could see the house, just to the left side of the road, in front of the crossroad. I quickly entered through the gates and with steps of a young man with a mission climbed the stairs leading up to the front door. I rang the bell. Had to wait for a minute or two. Then the old man opened the door, probably in his mid seventies, heading for eighty. I said good morning and quickly announced my business—I would like to rent a bike. The old man looked at me in silence. Just before it started to feel really creepy he said: "No, I have no bikes to rent to you". I was perplexed. I did see from where I was standing a hell of a lot of bikes just on the left side of the house so it could not be the wrong house. Then it hit me. I took a step back, took in some air, clearing my head, calmed down and asked: "How is life at Fårö?" "Well", the man said, "I will tell you..." We talked about this and that, small and big for about 15 min. Then suddenly the man said "You wanted to rent a bike, didn't you? I will give you a nice bike." And it was. I must say it was the best bike I ever rode, the premium bike, the one and only. So what did I learn?

Well there is no single nature of the story; one could learn many different things. What I did learn then, what stayed with me over the years as a clear insight was the following: I learned that money transactions such as those involved in renting a bike are just that; grounded on in-personal relationships, that is, on transactions having nothing to do with life. If you want to be dramatic about it you could say capitalism is not life. The man did not want just to rent out bikes, he wanted to talk to people, have a relationship with them, and he probably wanted to "teach" me something. Renting out bikes was secondary to all that. But whatever reasons the man had for acting as he was doing (or the nature of Capitalism in late modernity) something important happened in me. I realised that I had another person in front of me. Not just anyone but someone. And in order to see him I needed literally to take a step back and leave room and space for him to enter into the relation. I needed to give up my ego, my plans, my activity, and passively let the other appear for me as an other that was wholly outside me, an absolute other. But an other for me and no one else within the moment of the relation. That is, his otherness was my responsibility and no one else's. This recognition made me appear fully alive in the present of time. I was there and nowhere else, released from my ego but not from myself in being for the other. No wonder the bike ride was so good that day, the sky so clear, the sun so bright, and life so mysteriously rich and full.

Of course it is many years later I'm able to put those words to the event, after reading Emmanuel Levinas and thinking about what we often too easily call learning in education through his lenses. But my memory of my insight that day makes perfect sense for me now: If we with learning mean something fundamentally different from stocking up information, something that has to do with life it is a far more risky business than what is often portrayed as learning but also something much more beautiful. So maybe this is something for my pedagogical creed. *Learning is fundamentally about living a life in the presence of others in the present.*

Second Story: About Teaching

This story takes place in the war zone in Sri Lanka in 2000, in the town Batticola on the east side of the Island, then about 70 km behind the frontline. Sri Lanka's army controlled the town itself but the land surrounding it was a no man's land. And the town was just barely under control new posters about the Tamil Tiger 'freedom fighters' appeared anyway every morning on the town walls. I was in Sri Lanka to conduct a project for the Swedish international development agency (Sida), leading a team investigating the conditions for establishing a framework for future projects devoted to education for democracy. In my usual Monday morning meeting with the team analysing data, and discussing what the next step should be, I suggested that we needed to go also to areas deeply involved in the war. I found it important to do so in order to be as true as possible to the situation at hand. For me it was important since I thought I needed some kind of first hand experience of the conflict in order to better understand what was at stake for people in common in Sri Lanka. Sharmini, a Tamil woman on the team, was to accompany me into the warzone. We were stopped exactly 70 km outside Batticola at a heavily armed military checkpoint. They checked our papers and talked to Sharmini, opened the gate and off we went. The trip into town went smoothly. (Going back, however, was a total different story. We then witnessed an attack from an armed helicopter far out on the left side of the road, a road on which we were the only car for the entire 70 km stretch, the day after a military jeep was blown into pieces by a bomb on the side of the road, killing four soldiers. So the calm and quite beautiful ride into town was a blessing in comparison.) In the town itself we visited several schools, talked to parents, teachers and professors at the university. The university professors we talked to had projects with kids in schools in order to try to counter the trauma of war with drama and other ways of staying sane despite the insanity of what was going on. Sharmini and I were meeting a class of girls, 12 year of age, in one central school. The room was spacious and sunny, the girls sitting in a half-circle in front of us on dark wooden chairs in their blue and white school uniforms. We asked them about their experiences of school, their daily life and so on. After some small talk one of the girls stood up. She started to talk with a steady and strong voice, with a dead serious expression on her face, and with concentrated emotional intensity she looked straight into my eyes. She said: "I can die by an explosion or gunfire everyday I go to school and everyday I go home from school." Just like that. Simple. Straightforward. Someone speaking. It is just a sentence. But for me I just know that everything I was to do from that moment and on in Sri Lanka had to be a response to that sentence, to that girl, to do justice to her voice speaking. In her voice and in her speech was the entire complexity of the situation made into one simple and brutal truth, which fundamentally changed me.

How then do I understand this story? It speaks about the brutality of war, of the complexity of the foreign aid business, and about the sometimes all too idealistic hopes connected to schooling. Education cannot end wars or bring democracy to a country. That can only happen through people doing politics. But I also learned that despite what can be said about schooling as a process that only confirms an already ongoing socialisation rather than changing its conditions, nonetheless the place, the actual school, functioned as a safe place for particular kids in a particular situation. The school building, like any other building in town, could be hit by a bomb at any moment, but still, because of what was going on inside, the place meant something different for those kids and gave them a feeling of security. So secure that the girl could speak to me in her own voice. Still, the most profound learning I did in Sri Lanka is connected to the girl speaking. She was able to teach me, to speak right through my own preconceptions of the totality of the situation at hand by making it brutally real, direct, and inescapable. Through her speech separate worlds were connected. She changed the very context for how to make meaning of her words at the same time as uttering them. It was deeply affecting me. I was not any longer just hearing her words but was fundamentally moved out of place. It opened a possibility to understand something profoundly new about the situation in which I was implicated. In the speech that unmistakably came from that girl and no one else, she touched something that was unmistakably in me and in no one else. In the moment of speech there was equality in the sense that it reached beyond the social/historical/geographical positions from where the speaking bodies originated. In such speech we can hear the other speaking in ways that bring a certain kind of truth to the forefront. It is the very moment in which noise is turned into discourse and in which the sensible dimension of living a life changes so as not only to understand something new, but also to bring radically new meaning to the world.

The girl taught me something I did not see coming, her voice moved me out of place. It changed what were previously some self-evident facts for me in my world by confronting it with another world. To teach and to be taught, then is something fundamentally different from delivering ready-made schemes. It is about speaking in ways that change the distribution of the sensible in such a way as something can be seen and heard that was not heard or seen before by connecting different worlds. So maybe this is something important to add to my pedagogical creed. *Teaching is a particular way of speaking, a confirmation of a certain kind of equality through which noise is turned into discourse by connecting different worlds.*

Some Final Words

It seems like things I learn for real I learn on an island! Maybe that is why they say that every man is an island (which I think is a lot of rubbish anyway). It turns out though that my pedagogical creed cannot be separated from those stories/memories that make up a life and how those stories connect to systematic thinking in that life about how to live it. Thinking and acting are not easily separated. I am still at heart a pragmatist. Also I guess it is thinking and acting on real problems that keeps the world turning. It is by starting with real problems and sorting them out, I guess, which fundamentally make a life. Teaching and learning can be many things but if those events in a more fundamental way are related to life, and not only to how to make a living, then they are fundamentally about particular relations between people. So in teaching and learning no man or woman is an island, rather, essentially one is in relation to another that is not the same as oneself, that is, a relation to another person is a relation across difference. Striving to make the same out of difference is not life. It can be called capitalism, it can be called un-relational in this particular sense, it can be called every man is an island, it can be called how to make a buck, it can be called make a living, but it cannot be called to make a life. And for me it cannot be called education either. I do guess that education is strictly about how to make a life worth living together with others. The judge of that worth is my own and has something to do with speaking as if I have the right to speak even in situations discouraging me of that right, and maybe particularly in those situations. In the stories above, teaching and learning are somewhat interchangeable around a particular point, a point at which there is no learning without teaching and no teaching without learning. I guess this point can be called equality, but not without specification. For learning/teaching in Levinas's sense there is always an asymmetry in that I am always and absolutely responsible for the other, without any hesitation whatsoever and without any claim to the reverse. While for Rancière, there is no relation, at least no political and/or educational relation, if not based on an assumption of equality (in a situation of inequality). Saying that Levinas seek the moral point of view while Rancière seeks the political one can of course solve this dilemma, but only rhetorically and for the time being. What I am sure of, though, is that both of them brings something important to teaching and learning, and that is the idea of an absolute difference necessary for making a life and not only a living. With Rancière this shows most clearly I think in his politics in which he sees that politics is to divide Ochlos, the idea of society as a corporeal whole while in Levinas, as has already been touched upon, it is the asymmetrical relation to the absolute other. Despite their differences, what I bring to education, maybe as a dissonance, is the equality required for teaching and learning, which is not sameness, but an asymmetrical relation; teacher-learner, teacher *for* the learner not before him or her, is an assumption of the possibility of speaking, in its most fundamental meaning of speech, across difference, and of hearing that speech, of relating worlds. It is the idea that when we do occasionally speak, and not just talk, we do that from a place/position of absolute difference from everyone else, and that is precisely this difference that makes it possible to be heard, that is to relate to someone other than myself beyond the noise of common sense. Teaching and learning are not commonsensical. If so, it would only be repeating the same endlessly. Teaching and learning are not about making more sense, but about changing the sense. And when it occasionally does so, one is present for another at exactly this moment in this particular world.

Nurturing a Democratic Community in the Classroom

Barbara J. Thayer-Bacon

Published online: 20 April 2011
© Springer Science+Business Media B.V. 2011

Abstract Thayer-Bacon tells her story in a conversational tone that traces her personal and professional roots as she describes various chapters of her life: first as a philosopher, how she became involved in education, and then how that involvement became a career as a philosopher of education, in a large teacher education program, and now at a research institution. She sketches her philosophical contributions, as a pragmatist, feminist, postmodernist, and cultural studies scholar, to philosophy, philosophy of education, and education.

Keywords Feminism · Pragmatism · Postmodernism · Cultural studies · Marxism · Montessori

Introduction

I am a philosopher by nature. I don't mean that to sound like a brag, for my family would say it can be very frustrating to have a daughter, sister, parent, and partner who is a philosopher. As a child, I worried a lot about social issues and loved to analyze ideas. No one else in my family of origin claims to like to talk about social issues such as how to reform our schools. My family still can't figure out where I came from. Fortunately, I loved to read and had a library card I used. I also made friends easily. I found people willing to debate me and challenge my thinking.

I went to Penn State (The Pennsylvania State University) for college, which was a very opportune choice, as Penn State was one of the few colleges in the US at the time that emphasized continental philosophy, in particular existentialism and phenomenology. I am not sure I would have earned a degree in philosophy if I had been on a campus that

B. J. Thayer-Bacon (✉)
Cultural Studies of Education and Learning Environments and Educational Studies,
University of Tennessee, 1126 Volunteer Blvd, Claxton-420, Knoxville, TN 37996-3456, USA
e-mail: bthayer@utk.edu

emphasized analytic philosophy and language analysis. I don't think it would have caught my imagination in the same way. I took Dr. Alphonso Lingis's introductory course in philosophy, loved it, and signed up for more. I had no idea what I was going to do with a philosophy degree, except go on to graduate school in philosophy. I followed my heart, and hoped for the best. I was philosophizing before I earned a degree, and will be doing so long after I retire. I'm still surprised that someone is willing to pay me to do what I'd be doing anyway.

I start with this introduction for several reasons that have to do with my philosophy of education. One, I don't think philosophy should be elitist, and it bothers me that many people find it too abstract and disconnected from their daily lives to be worth their while to consider. I think many people are interested in philosophical ideas; they just don't label them as such. One key concern I have for philosophy is that philosophy needs to be approachable and available to all. Connected to this concern for approachability and accessibility is the strong belief that philosophy needs to help people solve real problems in their lives, be applicable, relevant, and useful. Our thinking has consequences; it is directly connected to action and needs to help improve our daily lives. That philosophical view is what makes me a pragmatist.

Third, I start with my voice being heard, as I am also a social feminist scholar who thinks the boundary between subjectivity and objectivity, as well as self and others, is very porous indeed. I do not think I can separate my private self from my public self, that I can remove myself from my context and step out of my own skin. My multifarious self is necessary for the construction of knowledge, it is not just something that gets in the way or deceives me. Feminists argue strongly that the personal is political, which brings me to point number four, the importance of addressing power and making sure diverse perspectives are included in the conversation. I did not read feminist philosophy in any course I took in college as an undergraduate or graduate student. Women doing philosophy was not part of the curriculum. I also wasn't introduced to postmodern theories concerning the relationship of power to thought until I was a doctoral student. It was Marxism, during the second half of my undergraduate degree, at Rutgers (Rutgers, The State University of New Jersey), that helped me to understand more about power. Still, the Marxist focus was on social class issues, and capitalism. I had to turn to feminist scholars in my outside reading and participate in the Feminist Movement to help me make connections to gender issues. I read books by Black scholars and participated in the Civil Rights Movement, to make my own connections to race issues.

Once I began to see injustice and inequality in our world, I couldn't help but see it. Once I realized I was privileged in some ways, because I was White and my father was a career officer in the Air Force, I couldn't help but see that my parents were better able to serve as advocates for me in school in ways that my enlisted friends' parents were not, while at the same time my high school guidance counselor had no expectation that I would graduate from college because I was a girl, and my parents saw no reason for me to continue in college once I married. I experienced gender discrimination directly in ways that helped me understand other forms of marginalization. All of the social context within which I grew helped me become the cultural studies scholar I am today. I understand my role as a philosopher to be a cultural critic. Let me turn my attention now to chapter two of my life, how I became involved in education, and then to how that involvement became a career as a philosopher of education in a large teacher education program and now at a research institution. I will sketch my philosophical contributions to philosophy, philosophy of education, and education in the process.

Chapter Two, Elementary Education

I married at the too young age of "almost 19" and finished my undergraduate degree in philosophy at Rutgers before I turned twenty-one. When I graduated I was 6 months pregnant with my first child of three that I had before I was twenty-six. I was also on my way to Germany, pulled away from the graduate school I thought I would attend and the philosophy I wanted to pursue. Consequently, I went back to relying on my library card and reading, as well as making new friends. My children sidetracked me in a very important way, as they pulled me into the world of education, at home and then in their Montessori school. I had no intention of being involved in teaching children prior to having children, considering that to be traditional women's work. Then, I started to worry about my own precious children's education. As I was living in Germany when my first child was born, I began to compare various ways of educating children in Europe to what was available in the US. I learned that there are many options for how to design a school and curriculum, something I had never considered before, and that was all my imagination needed to get me reading more and pondering various possibilities. During the time my children were growing up there was a strong push to develop alternative schools in America and parts of Europe.

When we moved back to the States I helped to develop a Montessori school so that my children could attend, and ended up going through Montessori elementary training so that I could teach in the school my children attended. Their joy in their school was contagious. I discovered teaching is the most challenging and rewarding job I can imagine doing and I still love it. When my children were old enough, I went back to graduate school, first earning a public school teaching credential, then a Masters in Education, both while still working fulltime as a Montessori teacher. Then, I learned about the possibility of earning a Ph.D. in philosophy of education. I was so excited! Here was a degree that would allow me to bring together my love of philosophy with my love of education. I felt like I had come full circle, and now that circle was complete.

Even though my children are grown, I still try to design my research so that I spend time in classrooms with children. My experience as an elementary Montessori teacher still informs my thinking. My (Thayer-Bacon 1991) dissertation was on critical thinking theory, in particular Richard Paul's theory in comparison to other current philosophers working on that topic. I was trying to understand why the children in my classroom scored so high on the annual proficiency exams I was required to give them, even though my curriculum did not match the public school curriculum for which the tests were designed. My hypothesis was that my students were using their critical thinking skills to reason out the most logical answer. Thus began my inquiry to try to understand what my students were learning and how they were learning *it*. In my research on Richard Paul's critical thinking theory, I found that what was significant about his theory for education was his requiring that the critical thinker become aware of their egocentrism and ethnocentrism. Such a requirement opens the door for others to be heard, and have their ideas considered before they are dismissed. However, I was disturbed by Paul's view of the self's contribution to knowledge in only a negative way, that the self can get in the way of knowledge obtainment, because it is selfish and self-centered. I began to develop a redescription of critical thinking that critiqued the current critical thinking work (Ennis, Paul, McPeck, Siegel, Lipman), and extended the current paradigm for thought in a new direction that incorporated feminist theory (Gilligan, Noddings, Ruddick, Grimshaw, Flax, Code, Jaggar), pragmatism (Peirce, James, Mead, Dewey), as well as postmodern theory (Habermas, Lyotard, Derrida,

Foucault, Rorty). That theoretical work was published as *Transforming Critical Thinking: Thinking Constructively* (2000).

I am currently working on developing democratic theory beyond liberal democracy in schools and once again Montessori's (1909/1912) model for schools and classrooms informs my thinking, in comparison to other models such as Dewey's (1990) Chicago Lab School and Horton's (1990) Highlander Research Center. I spent 5 years in schools with students whose cultural backgrounds have a more collective, "it takes a village to raise a child" focus, instead of the strong individualism so prevalent in American schools. I (Thayer-Bacon 2008) argue that individualism can be traced back philosophically to Locke and Rousseau and the classical liberal concept of 'democracy' America embraced from them. I am still absorbing my field notes from visiting nineteen schools on three different continents, and trying to further enlarge my thinking through reading as I continue to develop a relational, pluralistic theory of democracy-always-in-the-making.

However, I am getting ahead of my story. Chapter Three for me began when I took my first job in higher education as an assistant professor at a large teacher education program, Bowling Green State University (BGSU), with four children in tow, my oldest a senior in high school and my youngest a toddler. This is a woman's story, after all.

Chapter Three, Higher Education

I taught future teachers in Bowling Green, Ohio for 9 years, with a teaching style that was influenced by my years as an elementary Montessori teacher. I still teach this way, in my second higher education job at the University of Tennessee (UT). Montessori taught me that I am not the only teacher in the room, my students are teachers as well. She also taught me to trust that my students want to learn, and to let them choose what they will learn. Self-directed learning is the most powerful, in terms of engagement, motivation, and retention for the learner. I position myself as a student and try to help my students see themselves as teachers. I truly hope to learn as much from my students as they learn from me. I try to create a classroom where students feel safe enough to risk sharing their views, and I encourage them to listen, attend, discuss, seek alternative ways to look at issues, critique, and offer solutions. I consider us a democratic community of inquirers. We discuss ideas, in small groups, large groups, and now on line. I encourage them to discuss the ideas we look at with others beyond our classroom too, to help further enlarge our community of inquirers. I often serve as a translator for obtuse, difficult theoretical arguments. We read diverse scholars in every course I teach, and we read those scholars' original work, not secondary sources. I want students to feel confident they can engage with the ideas directly, and I want them to use care in making sure they are not misreading others' work. The only way to really test one's understanding of another author's work is to go back to the original writing.

The students do presentations about the readings as a way to break them down into reasonable amounts and share the responsibility for leading discussions. They write journals in which they describe, interpret and critique key points from their readings, position papers wherein they debate an author on a key issue, and longer philosophical papers where they develop their own ideas in more depth. I try to build into the curriculum and the writing assignments as much choice as I can. Same thing with our discussions, I come in with a basic outline of possible topics and issues, but I follow the students' interests and go where they want to go in our classroom discussions. There are always current events and examples that we can bring in to make connections, amend, and extend the ideas we discuss and write about. The students also bring in other scholarly connections from their diverse educational backgrounds.

I do not grade students on the positions they take, I grade them on their ability to be fair in their representation of the other scholar's ideas and clear in describing their own. I teach students to use what I call "caring reasoning" in our discussions in class as well as in their writing. As authors, we learn that we are responsible for being as clear as possible about what we want to say, so that others will not misunderstand us. Since language is ambiguous and continually changing, this is a very difficult task, but one in which authors must engage. When I taught at Bowling Green State University (BGSU) I encouraged the students to think about how learning to use caring reasoning was going to help them in discussions with their students' parents, as well as with their co-workers and administrators. They have to be able to show they can fairly describe the other's views with generosity, presenting the ideas in their best light, not their worst. Then they have to be able to present their own argument in agreement (extending the ideas) or in disagreement (amending the ideas). They have to imagine the other person's response, and take their concerns seriously, as they seek to address those concerns.

Now, at a research-one level university where I work only with graduate students, I tell my students to imagine the authors they are reading are in the room having a conversation with them about their ideas. I give students lots of feedback on their writing, and the opportunity to rewrite as often as needed. I encourage them to read each other's writing too. My method of assessment is a mastery approach, much like what I learned as a Montessori teacher. I try to put students' grades in their hands as much as possible, and let students work on their writing until they have mastered it. I become a writing coach. All my grades are "in pencil" until the end of the semester, and if a student runs out of time due to life encroaching in on them, I will give them an incomplete to provide more time. What I care about most is that they have the chance to do their best work.

In the classroom I do not hide who I am, just as I haven't here, and encourage my students to do the same in class and in their papers, at a level they are comfortable. At the same time, I encourage us to push ourselves into discomfort zones, as that is where real growth takes place. I rarely have students with strong backgrounds in philosophy. I also rarely have students who walk into my classes thinking philosophy is important and relevant to their lives. Many walk in feeling intimidated by philosophy. I (Thayer-Bacon with Bacon 1998) wrote my first book, with contributions from Charles Bacon, my partner, for my students at BGSU, to help them see the value of philosophy and how it contributes to education. I wanted them to understand that in fact they are dealing with philosophical issues all the time as classroom teachers; it is unavoidable.

I did not realize it at the time, but *Philosophy Applied to Education* has become an outline of my career, as I have developed several of the original chapters into other texts. I (Thayer-Bacon 2000) first worked on developing chapter four more, concerning critical thinking. I finally felt like I managed to describe what was going on in my elementary Montessori classroom that captured how students were learning to be constructive thinkers. When I was working on *Transforming Critical Thinking,* I realized I needed to develop further a relational epistemological theory that supports my description of constructive thinking. Thus, I (Thayer-Bacon 2003) turned my attention to epistemological theories more (chapter two), and wrote *Relational* "(e)pistemologies".

My relational (e)pistemological theory is a pragmatic social feminist perspective calling for active engagement, aiming at democratic inclusion, joining theory with praxis, striving for awareness of context and values, tolerating vagueness and ambiguities. Knowledge is something people begin to develop as they have experiences with each other, and develop ideas and understandings about what those experiences mean. A relational (e)pistemology views knowledge as something that is socially constructed by embedded, embodied people who are in relation with each other. It relies on a pluralist view of truths, not Truth as an absolute, which is why I place ( ) around the "e" in epistemology, as traditional Epistemological theories are based on a concept of Truth as Absolute. Like other feminists, pragmatists, and postmodernists, I do not believe philosophers have a "God's eye view of Truth."

I completed the first draft of *Relational "(e)pistemologies"* just as I was offered a new job at UT, thus giving me a chance to work with students seeking graduate degrees in philosophy of education as a specialization within UT's Cultural Studies in Education program. Cultural studies scholarship has pushed me further on understanding the categories of culture and race as well as sexual orientation, and helped me to make important philosophical connections beyond the boundaries of teacher education to include sports studies, community health, instructional technology, and now applied educational psychology, as I have worked with various colleagues from these diverse fields of study since arriving at UT.

I began further developing the application of my relational (e)pistemology through my research on community and caring in education, as I describe in section two. I started this social-political philosophical theorizing about democratic communities in the classroom once again in *Philosophy Applied to Education* (chapters one and five). This project has taken me to schools in countries as far away as China, Japan, Ghana, and Mexico, and as close as my own backyard (where there are schools with 90% + African American children). I also am working on writing essays about my experiences as a teacher, professor, and administrator that focus on caring as an ethical approach to education (*Philosophy Applied to Education,* chapter three). And, I have come to the realization that I need to address a void that exists in *Philosophy Applied to Education,* in terms of overt theory development, for I inadvertently left out a key branch of philosophy (metaphysics). I need the chance to think through at a deep level the warp of relational ontology that goes with the weft of relational (e)pistemology and forms the weaving of the net that is my relational philosophy, and philosophy of education. I continue to experiment with ways of presenting philosophical work that are approachable and accessible to "non-philosophers," such as using narrative stories, vivid metaphors, and a conversational tone.

Conclusion

I hope it is clear from my description of my teaching and research agenda that issues concerning equity are central to my work. As a feminist, gender is always part of my focus. However, as a social feminist with a pragmatic perspective my focus includes race, class, and other diversity issues. I am committed to the value and importance of understanding cultural diversity, and I embrace a democratic society always-in-the-making as the place where there is the greatest opportunity for social diversity to be valued. I am also committed to translating theory to practice, as a pragmatist, and this brings my work continually into the arena of public policy concerning these issues.

References

Dewey, J. (1990). *The school and society [1900], and the child and the curriculum [1902].* Chicago: The University of Chicago Press.
Horton, M. (1990). In H. Kohl., & J. Kohl (Eds.), *The long haul: An autobiography.* NY: Teachers College Press.

Montessori, M. (1909/1912). *The Montessori method*. NY: Random House.

Thayer-Bacon, B. (1991). *The significance of Richard W. Paul's critical thinking theory for education*. Unpublished doctoral dissertation, Indiana University, Bloomington, IN.

Thayer-Bacon, B. (2000). *Transforming critical thinking: Thinking constructively*. NY: Teachers College Press.

Thayer-Bacon, B. (2003). *Relational "(e)pistemologies"*. NY: Peter Lang.

Thayer-Bacon, B. (2008). *Beyond liberal democracy in schools: The power of pluralism*. NY, New York: Teachers College Press.

Thayer-Bacon, B., & Bacon, C. (1998). *Philosophy applied to education: Nurturing a democratic community in the classroom*. Upper Saddle River, NJ: Prentice Hall.

The Educational Thing

Thomas Aastrup Rømer

Published online: 1 May 2011
© Springer Science+Business Media B.V. 2011

Abstract In this essay, I argue that education should be conceived of as a thing in itself. To lift this view, I present aspects of Graham Harman's philosophy, a speculative realism that can be seen as a radical break with social constructivism and similar approaches. Next, I attempt to outline a rough sketch of an educational "thing", drawing on concepts such as protection, love, swarm, tension and shadow. Finally, I briefly discuss some implications of this vision for philosophy of education. In particular, I think that my discussion point to philosophy of education as the basic discipline in an educational science.

Keywords Speculative realism · Philosophy of things · Educational object · Heidegger · Harman

Over the past decade, Graham Harman has published several books that intend to turn much recent philosophy upside down. First, he wrote *Tool-being*—a peculiar interpretation of Heidegger's philosophy, positing all things' independent existence, and in 2005, the book *Guerrilla Metaphysics: Phenomenology and the Carpentry of Things*, on which I focus in what follows, appeared. Basically, Harman tries to develop what he calls a "speculative realism" or a "weird realism", portraying a world of objects that exist independently of our discourse and perception of them.[1] It is a return to a kind of essentialism. He describes a philosophy for things in their diversity and their essence, and he develops a way of thinking about things and their causality. These objects have their own lives from which we as such are excluded. Therefore, the objects can also accomplish surprising and strange things. This is why he calls this a "weird realism". He even speaks of "guerrilla metaphysics", a philosophy of a strange, independent and invisible world. Harman's work is not scientific or positivistically grounded—on the contrary. He writes in

---

[1] See Harman (2009, p. 334) for a discussion of this term. The other references in this paper are to Harman (2005), except where otherwise explicitly stated.

T. A. Rømer (✉)
Department of Education, University of Aarhus, Niels Juels Gade 84, building 2110,
office 241, Aarhus, Denmark
e-mail: thar@dpu.dk

and out of a phenomenological tradition, discussing not only Heidegger, but also Husserl, Levinas, Merlou-Ponty and Alphonso Lingis at length. Thus, he combines phenomenology and philosophical realism. It is a negation to social constructivism and "the philosophy of appearances"—in which objects are constituted by the way we perceive them or by our discourses—which Harman believes characterises much of the phenomenological tradition. To a certain extent it is a return to an older pre-Kantian metaphysical tradition—for example to the philosophy of Leibniz and Spinoza. It is a return to Reality with a capital R. In the following, I first present this phenomenological realism, then the contours of a speculative and "weird" object of education, and finally I suggest some consequences for educational philosophy.

Guerilla-metaphysics

A first point is that the realism of Harman is phenomenological and not positivistically justified. Objects in the world are not built out of minimal atomic parts or something like that. Things can be all sorts, for example a horse, a tent, a teacher, an education, Finland, love, etc. All the things we talk about, and which we use, are their own objects. So there is no ontological hierarchy. There is only a world filled with things. Yet, it is important to note that things exist in their own vacuous spaces. They are independent of our perception of them. They *are* in themselves, and they are closed around themselves in their own substantial existence. In this way Harman paints a picture of a world full of object-globes that float around in a metaphysical space. Even we ourselves are such globes. The world consists of spheres that attract each other and collide in different ways. As he says in connection with a discussion of "a tent": "The tent itself is an object, not a phenomenon" (p. 17). His attempt to turn philosophy around is also expressed in this statement: "The basic dualism in the world lies not between spirit and nature, or phenomenon and noumen, but between things in their intimate reality and things that are confronted by other things—with this single conceptual step, metaphysics is freed from its recent pariah status in philosophy" (p. 74). This means, among other things, that Harman is working with an absolute distinction between the object and our perception of it and he has, contrary to the Kantian tradition, the object itself as his primary focus.

Objects are sealed and isolated from each other. They are in the world like planets in the universe. The objects are essences. Harman praises ontology, essentialism and metaphysics; words that have been repudiated for many years in educational thinking. If there are objects, they must "exist in some sort of vacuum-like state, since no relation fully deploys them" (p. 81). Since the object cannot be fully described through sensory perception or social constructions, it must have its own existence, independent of these activities. "The objects in an event are somehow always elsewhere, in a site divorced from all relations" (p. 81). It is as if the object withdraws into a place which is always somewhere else. This site, this vacuum, is not physical but metaphysical. Thus: "To say that the world is filled with objects is to say that it is filled with countless tiny vacuums... What guerrilla metaphysics seeks is the vacuous actuality of things" (p. 82). So it is the character of "things" and their interaction that we are looking for; the things that exists for themselves, independently of human discourse. And this object is a hidden box full of surprises, never exhausted by the perception of other objects. That is why we can talk about "guerrilla". One is not bound by the paradigms or a particular social order. With a direct reference to Kuhn's paradigm Harman says: "It is always more interesting to meet explosive minds who oppose us wildly rather than cookie-cutter ideologues that happen to adhere to the usual views of our particular tribe" (p. 80). Things move us and touch us from their own site in the world, resulting—not in an abstract Heideggerian "wonder"— but in a collision of places in space that is capable of surprising.

Inside a closed object there is a world of its own: "Every object is not only protected by a vacuous shield from the things that lie outside it, but also harbours and nurses an erupting infernal universe within" (p. 95). In this universe elements are used in certain ways, as—in the vocabulary of Harman—"caricatures". A windmill, for example, consists of different parts (wings, wood, machinery etc.) but these parts are reduced to mean-end relationships within the overall purpose of a windmill. A "wing" could be caricatured by many other things (e.g. "to fly at the wings of liberty"). The object-globe of "wing", which may have drifted into many other things, in this case a windmill-globe, is turned into something quite specific in this new object. Thus, the "windmill object" is its own world of parts and a whole, its own substance that has absorbed elements from other worlds for its own purpose, its own existence. The windmill has become a "tool-being".

Harman then raises the question of how things are tied together. When things are not relational and when they exist independently of relationships, how can they come in contact with each other? What is it that causes a wing to become a part of a windmill or an individual to become a part of a people? How can an object become a part of our cognition? Or in one question: What happens when the globes collide? In this connection, Harman develops the idea of a "vicarious cause". A concept of causality he picks up from the pre-Kantian philosophy, where A does not act directly on B, but where both A and B act on each other because of an entirely different substance mediating between them. Things are brought together by a special ether, and when they bump into each other, an emotional and poetic plasma laps like a wave, and may form new shapes and structures. Harman calls the most central element in this ether "allure" (attraction/entice/charm). "Allure" is not only a physical but also a philosophical thing. It is not only a Newtonian attraction or feelings between a man and an object. Allure also work between the phenomenological objects themselves. Things bump into each other in hot and cold ways, forming nicks and accents. In my view, although Harman does not expand much on it, what is at stake here is the philosophy of Eros. You attract me is like saying that you are the object of my desire. This, in my opinion, brings the philosophy of Harman in contact with all the erotic philosophy, as expressed by Plato's Symposium and by many modern phenomenologists. Globes desire each other: both in the destructive sense of Sartre for whom Eros is both destructive and possessive, but also in the caring sense of Levinas, for whom Eros is warm and protective. Thus, bodies move around in an ether of desire, destroying and maintaining each other, producing new words and sounds and poetry.[2]

And "desire" detaches elements from the objects and links them to new objects. As when a woman goes from one marriage to another. She is the same woman but with a new "caricature", an element of a new marriage-object (but can the new husband discern "the woman" as an object in itself—an object which cannot be possessed, but must appear in this new "infernal universe within"?). Globes graze each other and exert attraction, which detaches elements from objects. When that happens, it is accompanied by sounds, voices and melodies, poetry, novels and emotions. We are a part of the "global" (globe = global)

---

[2] Harman is a very friendly reader to the late Heidegger lecture *The Thing* from 1949 (an essay generally overlooked, see for example Safranski's biography on Heidegger (Safranski 1998). In this lecture "a thing" is considered to be a mirror-play of Gods and mortals and between sky and earth: a fourfold (a concept which Harman uses himself). When the mirrorplay is fully at work, the "thing things" in a kind of glowing ring.

dance; a dance that is the objective origin of the phenomena. We are invited to a carneval, one of Harmans favorits words.

Finally, as already suggested, Harman has an interesting concept of "elements and moments". What happens when the attraction sets in, is that the detached elements of one object, are caricatured by another. Just as an electron can jump from one atom to another. As if, for example, "learning" jumps from the object of education to the object of economics. The word "elements" reminds me of Laclau's analysis from 1985 (Laclau and Mouffe 1985). He also distinguishes between element and moment. In his way of thinking, an "element" is a floating signifier, a word or a sentence lacking a discourse. A moment, on the other hand, is when the word is firmly established in a language game. Laclau is a social-constructivist of the radical kind. Harman transports this constructivist distinction between element and moment into the objects themselves. It is no more the battle of discourses, but rather the objects floating and colliding, that we are witnessing. Moreover, he makes a second switch. Whereas Laclau believes that the interaction between the element and moment is political-strategic, Harman tends to look at this interaction in the context of "allure". It is not necessarily something completely different, but certainly it is not the same either. I will not, however, go further into this comparison here.

The Educational Thing

What kind of globe is "education"? We would be wise not to respond too quickly to such a question. However, in terms of speculative realism, we must approach the question in metaphysical terms. It cannot be defined relationally or socially. "Education" must be expressed in terms of an object where "things" interact in ways that are entirely independent of empirical conditions. Afterwards, our "educational thing" may bump into other globes, for example an economic planet, a learning-planet or something else. I will mention three things we find when we look at the educational thing, as it is in itself, independent of all the people and words that happens by coincidence to be involved. Although the discussion is somewhat cursory, it should give an impression of the general idea.

First, we find love and protection—or care if you will. Education is protecting a public dialogue on topics you love. It is not private love that is the focus here. It is love for something in public, something you would like to pass on to all children (and not only to your own child) because it is meaningful in itself and because you cannot imagine a society without this knowledge or these values. This is true in the bigger picture, like when we for example talk about freedom and democracy. The reason that these words are in our school legislation is not that they are particularly rational or scientifically proven. It is because we have feelings about the freedom that was ordained by the constitutional events and developed by various popular movements from 1849 to today. But protection and love also matter on a smaller scale. Why are we sad when young people are not familiar with the names of towns and cities in their own country or region? Is it because a boy in Copenhagen needs to know about Hanstholm (a minor town at the other side of the Denmark) in a globalised economy? No, it is because Danish geography is linked to an area we love, where its dramas of freedom has appeared. We teach names of cities to protect Denmark (and Europe) because we love our country and our European and cosmopolitan origins. For the same reason we teach subjects such as literature, music and woodworking. This is to protect words, understandings and practises, that we believe are valuable in themselves, which need protection because they are not being disclosed by themselves. An uneducated parent may not his tell his son about European art. And I fail to pass on any pleasure in connection with crafts to my kids. But all children must experience the pleasures of both activities. Therefore, school must take over. School protects these activities because they are good and beautiful and important in themselves and for all. Teaching in this view is simply a defensive and protective activity that does not take into account special interests or special talents. When a teacher says: "Listen children", This amount to saying: "Our public community attach their love to these words and activities, a love that is protected by a popular-based law in a European cultural context".[3] Now, one can easily turn his feelings and his emotions and his protection in the direction of things other than a country or a European community (i.e. Asian industry or Mao's Cultural Revolution). The point is simply that love, protection and care are part of the educational thing.

The second element we notice when we look at the "thing" of education is myriads and appearances. Love and protection are linked to public and well-established traditions and understandings and dialogues, but it is also a defining feature of education that new children, students and pupils, bodies and faces constantly appear. Many new children from very different starting points and with different experiences and interests, acquire, correct and further develop what is publicly protected. If this "tumbling plurality" is forgotten, an authoritarian pedagogy may develop. It is only when we remember this new "throng" that education occurs. Pedagogy in this sense is the free interaction between new and the established dialogues. The new generations should not just blindly accept a hidebound basic order. They should instead swarm all over the place with texts, pictures, poems, songs and ideas. They must ask, suggest, avoid, fight, argue, disagree, laugh and cry. They must join together, split up, plunge, travel and remember. A new generation swarms and through their interaction with what is loved, they appear as new artistic or intellectual voices in the country. However, there is a problem here: If this "swarming becoming" does not occur within or on the edge of a public and protected set of issues that is surrounded with love by the majority, and is protected by school, the swarming generation will degenerate to self-centered, confused and selfish individuals who are far too dependent on screens, food and shopping. What is everyone's "ideality", one's desire to act in accordance to oneself in a community,[4] strays into closed and dreary spaces that people can spend a lifetime trying to orient themselves in and to get out of; a confusion that gives psychologists and diagnostics a field day. No, the teeming becoming can only develop as full active attention to the matter of culture in an atmosphere of public love for caring traditions. The school is one of the places where this whole cultural process of re-creation is structured and takes place. The school is a relationship between public love and a teeming becoming. And this relationship is complicated and unpredictable.

The third thing you find when you look at the thing of education is tension, which indicates that things should not come right; that the two already mentioned aspects of education (protection and appearance) cannot do without each other, but also must dispute each other. You cannot, in this view, do this or that and with evidence-based security be sure that something specific happens. Nor should we "build bridges" between theory and practice in teacher-education or avoid "shocks of practice". And one educational institution, for example a kindergarten, should not prepare for another: the school, which could prepare for college, which in turn should prepare for the university that is said to prepare

---

[3] This is completely in line with the view expressed by Hannah Arendt in her essay *The Crisis in Education* (1961).

[4] Socratic virtue in the context of the concept of "ideality", a concept I know from Danish poet, priest and life-philosopher Jacob Knudsen (1858–1917) (Knudsen 1907).

for business. We are not interested in coherence and unity, because these relationships do not exist in things themselves. When we look at the educational "thing", there is no research that will go around finding little quirky relationships between class sizes and test results, etc. Problems should not be resolved at all. Problems must instead be established; they must be established as resilient devices, as tensions in full diversity and thing-like ether. Thus, kindergartens (just as an example) are quite different from schools. They have other philosophical and practical roots and express different view of children's lives. If the kindergarten, which in Denmark has degenerated into a municipal service-centre and a school preparation plant, was fully itself and the school was the same, we would get two institutions that were as different as night and day, and kindergarten-workers ("pedagogues") and school teachers would play the music of a truly pedagogical difference (and we could add universities and folk high schools to this). This would create a wonderful tension in our culture, in every child and in every new generation; a tension that would stay in every one of us as a kind of urge, forcing everybody to speak and to become a voice in a public dialogue, a tension between a free gushing language on the one hand (kindergarten) and the relationship between swarming appearance and beloved public dialogues on the other (school). The same would be true regarding the relationship between school, college and university, which are also different things. It is the differences we must cultivate, so everything can be what it is. Thus, we should make things tricky and resilient to everybody growing into our entire educational life. This will give us plenty of problems, but not with the sad and lazy selfishness or with a general lack of public memory. Instead, we will get interesting and surprising ideas that pop up with a frank sense of the common good when the tension must be expressed as new appearances in science and culture.

A final example of the elasticity (the opposite of flexibility) and tension of the "thing" of education refers to the fact that every form of public protection and its associated swarm of appearances always have a shadow, a moon, a henchman, an anti-matter. Education is a double planet. That is the case because love is always a part of a dispute. For example, what is "Danish" is linked to the non-Swedish or non-German (and others) because the Danish globe has materialised out of a cloud of tension-filled material murmur. Something you love is formed together with its henchman/men, who always return as a rugged otherness. The educational thing is a double planet and its two moments, the main planet and its moons, keep each other in place by a *pugnacious magnetism* in a rugged attraction. This, in my view, is the field of thinking, the place between "is" and "is not", where thought can appear, where the world happens.

Thus, love, protection, swarming, appearance and tension are elements of the thing of education. That is the way a free people can appear in public attention and veneration for its common life and strife. It is the continuous formation of a new generation in the slightly battered, but still loving and warm image of the old.[5]

Some implications for philosophy of education

It should be noted that the various elements such as "swarm" may well have other meanings in other objects. "Swarm" can be tied to other attractions in other applications. But here, "swarm" is attracted by the object of education. "Swarm" and "appearance" are absorbed by and works together with the other elements (protection and resilience) in an

---

[5] See Rømer (2010) for an elaboration of this "object" of education. I think it can be developed on the basis of the heideggerian fourfold, se note no. 2.

object of education that is formulated on entirely essentialist grounds. Thus, there is an interaction between whole and part. There is an internal attraction, I think Harman would say. The educational thing is its own micro-universe, its own essence, its own globe. When this planet collides with, for example, a globe called educational administration, protection becomes rules. When the educational globe collides with an economic "thing", "swarm" is detached and transformed into innovation. If the collision is strong enough, an entirely new object, "educational economy", may emerge, where both the elements of economy and education are completely altered. The new ting is highly energetic and not static at all. The new things "things" as Heidegger says. It attracts other objects and makes them release signs of reality. On the other hand, the new thing may be forgotten. It may not "thing" at all, it may dry out and shrink. New things may cloud for the old thing, so it can hardly be sensed at all.

I have tried to make the description largely without references. I could probably have done better, but my point has been to emphasize the non-relational. It is not a knowledge that is constructed in *social* interaction with others (but in an interaction of *those who have nothing in common*). It is an attempt to look directly at things, in full attention. We skip all social attitudes and overlook all abstract methods. We should not tie one intelligence to another, as Rancière would have expressed it. I think we must return to a kind of erudite writing without references, to emphasize that one can see. It is as if thinking is in a strange contact with the rest of reality.[6] Both thought and reality are invisible, which is why they have something in common. They are made of the same invisible substance that can enter into specific kinds of metaphorical contact. When that happens, when a collision between the thing of thought and the thing of the world takes place, it results in strange, carnivalistic and unintelligible texts that return to the visible world like Socrates returns to the cave. That is what happens when the planet of thought collide with other planets. In Harman's words, the task of philosophy is to "listen closely to the faint radio signals emitted by objects—so as one night, alone, to hear what was never heard before" (p. 255). In other words, we should be careful that philosophy does not end up as being a social discourse; it is rather a certain kind of attention, an allure or Eros we share with the world.

Further, there is a point about the attraction that Harman believes both binds the objects together internally and makes them collide with each other. This attraction and these collisions have consequences, which are very similar to the "object of education" that I have just described. *Pugnacious magnetism* is a kind of attraction, and so are love and protection, and the whole relationship between protection and teeming appearance is in a sense a description of a "vicarious cause" that makes objects in the world to collide. The question is therefore whether the "educational thing" is simply the ether itself, the plasma that Harman is looking for? The world, perhaps, is moving in education. The world is education. Education is the ether that all other globes are moving in. Thus, Harman's work can be used to highlight the omnipresence of educational philosophy. Philosophy is not merely an academic discipline—it is also an ontological category. Philosophy is the world. The more you are part of the world's attraction and energy and the more you are immersed in philosophy, in the allure and the magnetism of things, the more you can see, think and feel.

Within this framework, one can easily engage in educational research, but it is obvious that one should distinguish sharply between educational research and education in itself. Education concerns the attraction, trajectories and collisions of the metaphysical objects

---

[6] The idea that thought and reality somehow comes from the same place is also found in the philosophy of Spinoza and of pre-socratic Parmenides.

and the internal cosmos of things. Research, on the other hand, is the registration of the visible consequences of collisions. Research is not about reality but about what you can see. Pedagogy, however, is about reality, and therefore it is invisible. Yet, sometimes it bumps into other globes, and the consequence is different kinds of perceptions and art. The idea that education should rely on evidence-based research is truly harmful, because such idea overlooks the fact that education is a real *thing*. What a proper educational science (and not just "educational research") would look like from this perspective is an open question. But at least it becomes possible, because it must build on something which is hidden but that also exists.

References

Arendt, H. (1961). The crisis in education. In H. Arendt (Ed.), *Between past and future*. Penguin Books: London.
Harman, G. (2005). *Guerrilla metaphysics: Phenomenology and the carpentry of things*. Illinois: Open Court.
Harman, G. (2009). On the horror of phenomenology: Lovecraft and Husserl. *Collapse, 4*, 333–364.
Knudsen, J. (1907). *Livsfilosofi*. Copenhagen: Gyldendal.
Laclau, E., & Mouffe, C. (1985). *Hegemony and socialist strategy: Towards a radical democratic politics*. New York: Verso.
Rømer, T. A. (2010). *Uddannelse i spænding—åbenhjertighedens, påmindelsens og tilsynekomstens pædagogik*. Aarhus: Klim.
Safranski, R. (1998). *Heidegger—between Good and Evil*. Cambridge: Havard University Press.

Going to the Heart of the Matter

Sharon Todd

Published online: 5 May 2011
© Springer Science+Business Media B.V. 2011

Abstract   Written as a conversational response to Rosa Luxemburg, this piece discusses the importance of going to the heart of the matter for education, seen here in terms of the actual flesh and blood subjects who are at the centre of a pedagogy of transformation.

Keywords   Rosa Luxemburg · Hannah Arendt · Luce Irigaray · Subjectivity · Aporia · Transformation · Becoming · Sexual difference

> Do you know what gives me no peace nowadays? I am dissatisfied with the form and manner in which people in the Party for the most part write their articles. It's all so conventional, so wooden, so stereotyped.... I believe that the source of this lies in the fact that people when they're writing forget for the most part to go deeper inside themselves and experience the full import and truth of what they're writing. I believe that people need to live in the subject matter fully, and really experience it, every time, everyday, with every article they write, and then words will be found that are fresh, that come from the heart and go to the heart instead of [just repeating] the old familiar phrases.
>
> Rosa Luxemburg, *The Letters of Rosa Luxemburg*

In her ever-restless spirit Rosa Luxemburg goes to the heart of what is needed if life is allowed to enter our theoretical prose and if our words are to capture something of the freshness of life. Her words speak at once beyond the commonplace, beyond conventional rhetoric and didacticism, beyond the prosaic formulas upon which writers come to lean. Coming from and going to the heart is not just about style, but a bodily engagement with text itself, a way of making life manifest, resonant with passion and commitment. In being offered this opportunity to write my own thoughts on education without the usual constraints of academic form means having to consider alternative modes of writing that, of course, bring their own constraints. But whatever the limitations might be—and the reader will no doubt be quick to identify them!—they are the necessary risks of intertwining

S. Todd (✉)
Department of Education, Stockholm University, 106 91 Stockholm, Sweden
e-mail: sharon.todd@edu.su.se

G. J. J. Biesta (ed.), *Making Sense of Education*, DOI: 10.1007/978-94-007-4017-4_12,   79
© Springer Science+Business Media Dordrecht 2012

writing with living, of writing not simply *as though* life mattered, but writing *because* it does.

What strikes me about the quote from Rosa—forgive the familiarity, for that is how I have addressed her for the past 30 years in my own imagined conversations with this formidable woman—is that it is every bit as much about education as about writing. For what she is calling for is not simply the overcoming of our stale or clichéd phrasing, which can position our texts as being way past the due date of the contemporary, 'real' circumstances we frequently write about, but an attention to the felt and experienced aspects of life as being important for thought. What concerns me here then is that writing my thoughts *on* education is really about writing my thoughts *in* education and finding a 'proper' mode of saying that captures how I interact in the world. This mode can only be for me one of response. A response to an address, to a text, to a person. An attempt to think through education as a response to another's call to respond.

****

I know what you mean, Rosa. Dissatisfaction with words, with their failure to live up in some ways to the demands of the world. What you have always taught me, although I have some questions regarding what you have sacrificed, is that passion is never far from the surface of political life. You longed to retire to Switzerland amidst the mountains and meadows with Leo, your comrade in arms, revealing the doubleness (perhaps the multipleness?) of what is at stake in thinking life alongside your desire. How one writes about justice and how one lives it is no simple task, and sometimes they pull in opposite directions. For instance, what has always interested me theoretically about justice in education has always been inseparable from my own educational experiences. How they use to deny the importance of my class and my being a girl, Rosa! Yet, even though my schooling has left its particular imprimatur on my life, there is no seamlessness between what I write and how I live or teach—a seamlessness captured in such well-worn phrases as 'walking the talk,' 'practicing what you preach'. These are the clichés I know you so despise—quite rightfully so. They seem to assume that there is no messiness or complexity in becoming transformed by ideas, or in acting in sync with our thoughts. As Hannah would say, there is no direct connection between our thinking and our actions, and although she would not have been revolutionary enough for you, Rosa, she nonetheless could appreciate the felt dilemmas of living a life politically engaged and passionately committed. But more than this, it is precisely this disorder that so characterizes our attachments—ethical, political, emotional—which is the very stuff of what transforms us, and what compels us to become someone different than before. But what a pedagogy of transformation means is not nearly so clear-cut for me as it possibly is for you.

Indeed, this is one of the tensions, I think, between us. Let's face it, it is not just party hacks but a long tradition of enlightenment ones—going back to the Greeks—that see education as an *instrument* for change, as something one needs in order to become someone other, someone altered: in your phrasing someone useful, someone who can carry on the fight. Why is this so? What makes you think that education ought to be put in the service of your political ends? Don't we simply end up in a theory of education as imposition, not unlike the most conservative theories of upbringing? Don't get me wrong, I know how unavoidable all this is. I stand up in the class, with my own (often implicit) desires, wanting the students to get something from the course, to change and alter not only *what* they think, but also *how* they think, introducing them to new possibilities that provoke their curiosity and, hopefully, new insights. At the same time, I try—really try—not to impose my ideas. I put on different hats, try on different guises in order to disrupt their thought, their conventional modes of address. "But," you will say, "is this 'side-stepping' really all that different from business as usual? Do you really think you can avoid your own influence, your own imposition?" Well, I suppose that is the point. I feel caught in what I see as the inherent ambivalence of education: we want to educate for change but we want to do so by ensuring what students become. As my good colleague Lars says in relation to Kant, the paradox of education lies in its treatment of freedom. Wanting desperately for students to become free while also wanting to form and mould them. What kind of freedom is this? So, I've always wondered, Rosa, how and if we can keep a sharp political eye on changing things while admitting of this paradox. How can we learn to live better in this *aporia* of education? I'm afraid I've become a bit obsessed by this question.

But what is this talk of *a poros*—without passage? Isn't the desire to change things about finding a passage, a road, a path that can help us navigate through the hazards of life? Shouldn't education at a fundamental level be about 'passage'? About finding one's way? About pointing students in the right direction? It is the certainty, Rosa, embedded in the idea of 'passage' that I am most weary of. There is a sense in which your dissatisfaction for wooden phrases resonates with my own dissatisfaction with wooden certainties that are so rife in education. How many times have people found *the* aim or *the* purpose of education as *the* answer to a wide variety of problems: poverty, illiteracy, sexism, racism—take your pick. Obviously, these ills ought not to exist and education needs to find a way of responding to them politically—and ethically. But to treat education as a political instrument can be risky because it can produce a non-thinking attitude to questions that demand our thoughtful, urgent attention. Seeing the passage too clearly *for* others robs them of their sense of sight and doesn't teach them to trust their senses, to feel their own way along, to reflect on their implication in the world. Imposing a passage can simply be a way of inviting resistance, which in turn deepens, not unexpectedly perhaps, one's own entrenchment in one's position. To get us out of our ensconced positions, we need to find the appropriate response to these issues in ways that do not instrumentalize education, and do not cement our certainties, but that turn education itself into a response—a response oriented toward the actual persons we encounter and the collective struggles they face. Perhaps you know this already, Rosa. You know the damage that can be done when we channel our energies into developing 'isms' (and education is full of them, let me tell you), at the expense of listening to others, at the expense of thinking itself. You either follow the passage defined by others or you are out. You know how this game works. You were murdered for it. Have we learnt nothing?

But this is sounding like a bit of a lament. And I certainly haven't spent most of my life in classrooms and other places to do with education because I think them useless, ethically bereft or politically meaningless. Being critical of 'isms', of the piety that surrounds our political aims of education, does not mean being derisive of education itself or of the ways in which it can make a difference in people's lives. But I do think, Rosa, we cannot be naïve about the *aporia* and felt dilemmas of schooling, even as I think education is fundamentally about change and transformation. But my question is: what transformational role can education play in order to make a difference in the world if it already presumes to know what it wants that world to be and what it wants students to become? Isn't this simply a function of arrogance? An arrogance that claims in the name of others how they ought to live and what they ought to value? How might we instead introduce humility into education in such a way as it can open itself up toward an indefinite future at the same time as it takes a stance toward past and present injustices? My own take is that unless we learn to live better in the *aporia*, we diminish education's potential and actually reproduce the very forms of imposition we seek to challenge, despite our best intentions. This means being

cautious, hesitant and mindful of our tendencies to define for others what 'we' think 'they'
need. Education and politics are not synonymous, and each sphere brings with it its own
responsibilities and dilemmas. There is definitely a place for politically informed pedagogical practices, but only without the vanguardism, without the knowing beforehand the
kind of world that will—indeed must—belong to a new generation. It is they, not us, who
have the right to define what their world will be; how it will be governed, organized,
thought about, experienced. But as Hannah pointed out so eloquently, if we lose sight of
the dilemma of education, caught as it is between past tradition and an indefinite future,
then we have no way of thinking in the present. Thinking *along with* a new generation,
being moved by their concerns and introducing them into ours. A present of humility borne
in a relationship of listening, reflecting, and judging. There is no room here for vanguardism, no place to tell others that they must be what we tell them to be; instead there is
a space that recognizes how I am bound to and separated from others in a complicated
drama of which I do not know the final act.

This, I think, is the 'truth' of the matter—the 'heart' of the matter. You once quoted
Lessing, a man whose sensibility also captured Hannah's imagination for his insight into
the relation with truth: "One who thinks of conveying to mankind truths masked and
rouged, may be truth's pimp, but has never been truth's lover." So if we may be permitted
to speak of a truth here as a lover, it has to be a truth without certainty, a truth that holds
surprise, a truth that cannot be prostituted for profit. For a lover simply could not do
otherwise to her beloved. She cannot tell her loved one how to change so she may love her
better. And such a 'truth' is about the uncertain event of education, the pedagogical event
of transformation that is occasioned not by government decree, or political will, or moral
imperative, but by what I see as a sometimes mysterious, almost alchemical, process
involving persons, places, and times. So going to the heart of the matter for me, Rosa, is
about going neither to socio-politico structures nor to psychology, but to encounter and
context.

It has to do with that lived experience you talked about—the one that ought to inform
our writing. Encounters are not simply about two people meeting, but about a calling forth
of our very existence in response to another, to others. Encounters with others are an
indelible part of both making and living a life. The *aporia* of education resides, then, not
only in the question of freedom and defining for others what their future ought to be, but
also in the relational ties that constitute my being present with and for others. Thus I am
also torn to some degree between *what* I am—a teacher—and *who* I am, which can only
unfold in an encounter with another. For this reason, I do not see that who we become, as
Hannah puts it, is reducible to what we are (including our class, our gender), neither is it a
purely individual, psychological process. Instead, these encounters are eminently 'social',
dynamic, and unpredictable. They are what make each of us unique and singular, like no
other. So when you and I talk politics, Rosa, I am thinking of the ways that we articulate
ourselves into being, through speech and action, through language and the body, through
narrative and drama as eminently political articulations in encounters with others. The
question then is how to accommodate such encounters into our educational schemes? How
to make room for the embodied 'who' to come forth in order to disrupt the hegemonic
assumption that education has always to be about developing a 'what'?

In some ways this is a profoundly feminist question, since it seeks to refuse already
defined identities, which as we women know have historically left us short-changed (at the
very least). This leaving open of the question of 'what' I am speaks directly to how social
identities rarely capture any sense of 'who' I am. And as Luce says, because we live not
only with capitalist greed but with patriarchy's desire, who 'I' am raises different stakes for

both women and men. For the question of subjectivity is not just a 'women's' question, but one that affects both sexes. It is based on the matrix of embodiment, language, and our relations to each other. So rather than speaking of replacing one identity with another, the point is to create an appreciation of subjectivity that is not yet defined, not yet filled with content or substance. This means that women's and men's subjectivities—and not their identities—are always becoming, are not-yet. This seems to me crucial, Rosa, in coming to understand that what lies at the heart of the matter are not simply different forms of identity, like shapes cut out of cardboard, but flesh and blood women and men embodying their emerging subjectivities. Allowing ourselves to think about the heart in this way means having a respect for the other's becoming. Educationally speaking, it means attending to pedagogical space in a way that treats education neither as a means to an end, nor as an end in itself, but as an unpredictable site, where we cannot know with any certainty what the future holds and which subjects will unfold in its midst—subjects both unique and different, in relation.

If each is not unique, then there is no plurality, there are no women or men, only abstractions: woman, man. In this I agree with Hannah, plurality is simply the human condition that we must face. If we see that each of us becomes someone as an instance of singularity, do we not have more of a chance to rearticulate a politics that respects the difference upon which our very existence rests? And if we see this process as pedagogical, then do we not have a sense of education that truly responds politically to current issues, as opposed to being an instrument of a politics always already defined elsewhere and by someone else?

As you know, Rosa, I'm not just speaking here of politics, but of an ethics that is part of the scene of transformation, the scene of pedagogy, the scene of becoming. I sometimes don't know where one ends and the other begins, but I do know that they speak to different aspects of our existence: our obligations to others, in the plural, and our responsibility for the other, in the singular. It is these two aspects that cannot easily be married. I somehow feel, though, that in your call for a political language that embodies the freshness of life, it is this level of specificity we find in the singular that can give us a grammar (if not a vocabulary) for animating our political concerns. This, I want to say, is also true for education. So long as we think abstractions can serve as substitutes for actual women and men, girls and boys, and that imperatives can stand in proxy for the future, then education will never be responsive to who they are here and now. That is, if we keep insisting on defining what they ought to be, according to our plans for their future, then we can never notice who each one is becoming, in context with others. It is not about having knowledge about our students that matters, but listening to them, attending to their presence revealed through the words they speak. The very power of the ethical, as I see it, comes from what you have called the 'heart'—the place of passion, warmth, affection, tenderness. Responsibility is born here, fragile and delicate at the same time as it is exacting and demanding. A burden, Levinas calls it, one that finds me wherever I go, one that speaks through me, whether I choose it or not. Isn't this the place of unique election that compels me to speak out against the injustices done to my neighbour? Isn't this a responsibility that can help us live better within the *aporia* of education, with attentiveness and awareness, with thoughtfulness and responsiveness? To me, it stands as a reminder of the price that is to be paid when we turn education into a faceless enterprise, into an 'ism', into a factory for identity production. We lose the idea that education concerns actual persons, women and men, who are always becoming present in context.

It is getting to be night and it sometimes feels to me as though I am warring with forces far greater than I can shed light upon. Quality, managerialism, performativity, accountability, excellence, impact factors, standardization, learning outcomes. The list is endless and it makes me tired, makes we wonder what a strange Vonnegutian system education has become. But so long as, I suppose, we can teach and write and learn with words that breathe, then the heart of education has perhaps not evaporated, but hangs fragrant and dewy waiting for new day, a new generation. Perhaps this is my Switzerland, Rosa.

Two Educational Ideas for 2011 and Beyond

Charles Bingham

Published online: 19 May 2011
© Springer Science+Business Media B.V. 2011

Abstract   In this article, I argue that education has come to a crossroads. It is so easy to become educated that the role of the teacher can be seen as redundant. Because of this fact, it is time to reconsider what the teacher does, and whether the aim of clear communication by the teacher can, or should, be an educational goal. I argue that clear communication can no longer be embraced. Instead I offer two new educational ideas for 2011 and beyond. One is that the teacher's role should be a relational role. The other idea is that the teacher's speech should be poetic rather than informative.

Keywords   Education · Communication · Teaching · Online information · Speech · Aesthetics

Two Educational Ideas for 2011 and Beyond

To speak about educational ideas for 2011 might be to speak about what the year 2011 has had to offer in terms of educational ideas. Or it might mean speaking about how educational ideas have changed as 2011 has arrived. And these two ways of approaching educational ideas in 2011 would consist of looking at the newest thought in education at this point in time. But I would rather speak about something different with regard to 2011's educational ideas. Namely, What should educational ideas for 2011 be?

For, I find that the particular juncture of 2011 has brought changes in technology and communication that force us to take new educational ideas more seriously than ever. Simply put, the year 2011 is witness to momentous changes in the availability of what can be easily accessed and learned online. It has become terribly easy to become educated. Education is, in a sense, everywhere. Unfortunately, education's everywhere-ness has not yet become a general cause for rethinking educational ideas. Educational ideas have tended to remain the same up until now.

C. Bingham (✉) .
Simon Fraser University, 1371 Borthwick Road, North Vancouver, BC V7K1X9, Canada
e-mail: cwb@sfu.ca

In this article, I make the case that there is a clear mandate for rethinking education ideas of today. And I will promote two such educational ideas—the idea of relation and the idea of poetic teaching. As I will argue, a mandate for such ideas does not come from educational theory nor does it come from educational practice. It comes from the year 2011 itself. It comes from the events that we will experience now and in the future with regard to easy access of knowledge and information.

Intensified Progressivism

As education has become more and more available, educational ideas have stayed pretty much the same. While vast changes in the availability of knowledge have made knowledge easily and quickly accessed by all people, still, many teachers, professors and educational institutions seem determined to do more of what they have always done, only intensified. One hears statements like this in 2011: "Educators must become increasingly flexible in their ability to meet the growing demands for knowledge in our knowledge-based society," Or, "It is nowadays the educator's job to sift through vast stores of knowledge in order to develop curricula that are streamlined and efficient." Or, "Today it is the role of the educator to be a 'guide on the side' while students access knowledge for themselves." Or, "Education is now more important than ever because we live in an information age rather than an industrial age." Each of these statements reveals the general sentiment that education must be intensified because information has become intensified. And, they share an underlying theme that progressivism is the best way for the 'new' educator to operate. An intensified progressivism is said to be the way of the future.

Upon closer scrutiny, however, this new call for the *same* educator to keep a hand on technology and information includes an unfortunate set of contradictions. First, if knowledge is easily and quickly accessed by *all* people, then the educator becomes a means of *slowing the student down* rather than enabling the student's capacity. Second, the educator's role, while perhaps intensified, also becomes *redundant*. Redundant, because informational algorithms themselves have proven quite successful at sifting through knowledge. The teacher is, more often than not, an outmoded analog cousin to such digital algorithms. Third, asking educators to respond to increasingly unwieldy networks of knowledge, or to respond to the ways that students negotiate such networks, is bound to lead to an impossible hyperactivity on the part of educators. Intensified progressivism will never be able to slow down because it will always be catching up. Thus, more-of-the-same actually makes no sense at all in 2011 given the above contractions.

Why Such Intensified Progressivism?

One must ask, of course, why these contradictions are so often overlooked. Why is there such a fixed and steadfast belief that intensified progressivism is the way of the future in education? The answer to this question lies in the following situation that confronts us in 2011: There is a general trend in the overdeveloped world to treat each and every human practice as if it can become part of school. One might even say that the overdeveloped world is *becoming a school.*[1] Wherever there is a new human practice, or a new production of knowledge, there is a rush to teach this new practice or knowledge. This process of

---

[1] Gert Biesta and I have described this in 2010, pp. 145–157.

becoming a school entails a few components. First, it is taken for granted at this historical juncture that everything that can be thought can also be curricularized. That is to say, if there is new knowledge, there must be a way to package such knowledge in an orderly form for consumption by students. Next, it is taken for granted that all knowledge that *can* be taught *should* be taught. So once knowledge is curricularized, once it is ordered and subjected to method, then it exists in such a form that it can be taught. Not only *can* but *should*. There is currently an unquestioning belief in the goodness of teaching, a belief that teaching whatever can be taught always has its place in the ideal world.

Add to this situation one more aspect—that of language or communication. It is this aspect that I shall focus on at length in order to offer some counter-ideas that rub against the grain of our overdeveloped world *becoming a school*. Working hand-in-hand with hyper-curricularization, and with the idealist belief in the goodness of teaching, there is a belief that language is the primary tool to be used to convey what has been curricularized. Language, it is generally assumed, works on the sender-receiver model. That is to say, human speech is assumed to convey—as if by pneumatic tube—meaning from one person's head to another person's head. Or, as I like to say, language is that magic means for taking ideas from the blood-and-guts of my brain and inserting them into the blood-and-guts of your brain. Following this model, the educator's role is to use his or her language to deliver curriculum to the student. There must be an educator, it is said, so that he or she can serve to explicate the ever-increasing stockpiles of human thought.

In short, two trends are converging on one another. On the one hand, there is an uncontrollable explosion of knowledge sources. On the other hand, there is deep belief in the organization and delivery of knowledge—in the form of curriculum, through the medium of language. At the intersection of these two trends rests the teacher who must be more and more knowledgeable, and who must speak more and more clearly about what he or she knows.

Theoretical Limitations

Now to focus more specifically on the matter of language. If I used a somewhat vivid metaphor of blood-and-guts earlier, it was to intimate that I find the sender-receiver model of language completely flawed. Indeed, many educational theorists have, over the past few decades, critiqued the sender-receiver model on various grounds. Using hermeneutic, Derridean, Foucaultian, performative, post-structuralist, psychoanalytic, and relational theory, educational thinkers have argued that language should not be understood on the sender-receiver model. And, many have argued that we should change educational practices precisely because language does not do what it is generally thought to do. Language does not transmit ideas from one head to another in any simple way. Instead, language enacts power, misunderstandings, unconscious slips, relation, and performative iterations just as readily as it transmits ideas—if it does transmit ideas at all.[2] If this is the case, then one should change education in order to better accommodate the messy and un-anticipatable effects of language. One should stop asking questions like "Did I communicate my ideas well to my students?" and "Did my students understand what I was saying?" Why? Because language does not, for the most part, communicate ideas nor does it, for the most part, promote understanding. One must instead be ready to give an educational account of the *surprises* that language has in store for us.

---

[2] I offer one of these sorts of linguistic critiques in Bingham 2002.

Unfortunately, very few educators, if any at all, have been ready to change educational practices following this critique of language. The problem with this critique is that it has remained a *theoretical* critique. The common sense version of language remains the sender-receiver model, and common sense understandings are notoriously resilient to theoretical insight. Indeed it feels like spitting into an ocean when one tries to talk to teachers and professors about the inevitability of *mis*understand and *mis*communication in education. Thus in stark contrast to the recommendations that follow from a theoretical critique of language, the effective speaker remains the bedrock of intensified progressivism.

The Event of Mute Teacher

But in 2011, if one looks outside of educational theory and educational practice, something else is also happening. It is happening without any heed being paid to the rhetoric of intensified progressivism, and without heed to the figure of the knowledgeable speaker. It is this something else that I want to emphasize. This something else might be called *The Event of the Mute Teacher.*

I offer this one simple example. On the web page entitled "Khan Academy," one finds the following message: "Watch. Practice. Learn almost anything—for free." And under the Khan Academy logo, "44,942,989 lessons delivered" is proudly displayed (Khan 2011a). Also on the web page is a link to a video wherein Bill Gates touts the importance of Khan Academy. "What Sal Kahn has done," notes Gates, "is amazing....

> He's taken all this material and broken them (sic) down into little 12 minute lectures. I use it myself to remind myself of things. Children like it. So I was super happy when he came up and we got to talk about—Where does he go now? How can my foundation help him pursue this dream, and connect it up with the other great things going on on the internet?... So I see Sal Kahn as a pioneer in an overall movement to use technology to let more and more people learn things, know where they stand. It's the start of a revolution (Academy 2011a).

Khan Academy consists of thousands of video clips that enable one to teach oneself whatever one wants. And as the website boasts, these videos are free, they are of high quality, and they can certainly do what they say they can do. They enable anyone to learn anything. Admittedly, the Khan Academy is more heavily focused on math and science. Admittedly, too, the academy, with its sequential staging of online pedagogy, has a sort of pre-modern, hyperrealist understanding that knowledge is something 'out there' written on some cosmic tablet. But it is not at all my aim to critique the web site, nor its epistemological assumptions. My point is rather to offer the Khan Academy as one example of thousands of other such places where one can become educated *other than* in a school or a formal educational institution.

Now, if we layer these sorts of pedagogical spaces onto the figure of the speaking teacher who finds it necessary to communicate ideas and to be well understood, we find that the well-spoken teacher is not really necessary in this year of 2011. What I mean by this is that there are thousands of speaking teachers available at anyone's fingertips, and it is very likely that the teacher one encounters at school or at university is *less* knowledgeable and *less* clear-spoken than another teacher who can be found online. For each teacher, there are quite a few Khan Academy's. It is in this sense that I say that the event of the mute teacher is upon us. There is not much need any more for the teacher to speak clearly. As Khan Academy boasts, "Views: 24,000,000. Faculty: 1" (Khan 2011b). Others are always at hand to speak for him or her, and to speak better.

A Practical Return to Theory: Relationality and the Art of Teaching

Importantly—and this is the crux of what I have to say about educational ideas in 2011—this event of the mute teacher forces one back into a situation where there is a choice to make between three options. First, one can cling to the sender-receiver model, emphasizing communication and clarity—and thereby hallucinate away the fact that the teacher does not actually need to speak in such a way any more. Such is the case at present. Second, one can cling to the Kahn-type model and decide that there is absolutely no need for the teacher. This is unlikely to happen given the ubiquity of educational institutions and their place in the structure of overdeveloped societies. Or third, one can reconsider an account of speaking that does not have to do with clarity of understanding. It is this third option that yields my two educational ideas for 2011.

Relationality

The first idea is this. The language of the teacher need not be communicative, nor need it be aimed at clarity. It can rather be considered a matter of relationality. Stripped of its propositional content, language still does something. It works at the affective level to form bonds of human connection (and, of course, sometimes to sever those same bonds). As I have argued elsewhere, relationality is much more central to the educational endeavor than what we learn or how we learn it.[3] Why do schools remain if not for meeting? The very existence of schools is surprising. In this age of books, libraries, TV, DVDs, and the internet, schools are not the only place to get information. Why do schools remain? They remain because education is primarily about human beings who need to meet together, as a group of people, if learning is to take place. In schools, it is true that we meet and it is true that we learn. But education is primarily about human beings who meet. Education and meeting are inseparable.

So one educational idea for 2011 consists in reclaiming the relational role of the teacher. For, while education is truly available in abundance in 2011; while there are phenomena like the Khan Academy wherever one looks—nevertheless, there remains a fundamental difference between a school and any other sort of educational resource. When people come *together* to learn, this is different than when they learn online or in libraries. In a school, there are teachers. And teachers *relate* to their students. That is to say, teachers are not necessarily destined to be mute in this day and age. The teacher still has the role of one who creates the circumstances for belonging and meaningfulness. When a teacher is in a classroom, he or she has the crucial human role of drawing people together. Without the teacher, a school is just like any other of the myriad places people can learn. With the teacher, the school can become a community.

The Art of Teaching

The second idea derives from a reconsideration of what is *said* by the teacher. For, while it is easy to slough off language as purely relational, there does remain a content to

---

[3] I describe this relational role of school in Bingham 2008, and Bingham and Sidorkin 2004.

speech. Such content must be dealt with carefully if it is not to return to the status of some 'clear,' explanatory speech that might as well be mute. I propose a reconsideration of the poetry of the teacher's words. When the teacher speaks, it is not necessary to consider his or her speech as the explanation of ideas so widely available elsewhere. One can instead consider what the teacher says as the translation of an experience. Such a translation is no different than the work of the artist, and, in particular, the work of the poet. To examine teacherly translation, consider the following poem by William Carlos Williams (1923):

The Red Wheelbarrow

so much depends.
upon.

a red wheel.
barrow.

glazed with rain.
water.

beside the white.
chickens.

The poet offers us the presentation of an experience. He offers us a wheel barrow, rain water, and white chickens. These artifacts, whether they are imagined or real, are experienced by the poet and a work is created. An experience is translated into a poem and the poem is available for translation by the reader. The poet does not explain or make clear a wheel barrow, or rain water, or white chickens. It is not as if there were such a thing as a particular barrow, a particular drop of water, or a particular chicken that might be clearly understood in a general sense. And the reader of the poem is not called upon to understand exactly what the poet has in mind. The reader is rather left to *counter*-translate the poem into his or her own experience. The reader will render the barrow, the water, and the chickens intelligible as best he or she can *without* the aid of the poet him or herself. While the poet has endowed the poem with meaning, such meaning is not delivered by the sender-receiver model of language. The words of the poet have a life of their own that defy explanation, a life that will be *shared* by the reader but not *understood* by the reader.

It is thus that the teacher need not be mute, even if education does not really depend upon the teacher any more. Indeed, we are at an important crossroads in this year of 2011. We are witnessing a time when the old adage that "teaching is an art" can be understood in a way that is more relevant than ever. Teaching must become an art in 2011 because teachers are now called upon to speak in ways that are more genuine and more poetic than ever. And when I say that teaching should become an art, I do not mean that art is a good metaphor for the way we teach. I mean something much more profound. I mean that we should speak in artistic ways. I mean that our work should intervene in life rather than describe life. I mean that we should offer renditions of life to our students. Renditions that are our own, not anybody else's. We should offer poetic utterances for our students to savor.

That The Classroom Might Become a School

In a way, of course, these two ideas of 2011—relational and poetic—are very old ideas. If we think back to earlier times, and to earlier educational practices, there is a sense in which the teacher used to be, once upon a time, in a position to act relationally and speak poetically. Even the word "school" depends on a more poetic connotation than it usually carries nowadays. School is more than a building. It is a place where people relate to one another under the guidance of one who speaks in a unique fashion. It is, according to the history of the word, a place of leisure. Today, of course, we have replaced this older notion of school with a modern version of the assembly line, where certifications are churned out. The school is a series of classrooms, each classroom having its own specific purpose in the production process of the finished product, the graduated student. Of course, the very word "classroom" demonstrates what is lost in this assembly-line transformation. "Classroom" is a redundant word that makes no sense at all. It means "room-room." In our "class-rooms" we find "textbooks"—another redundant word of nonsense, meaning "book-book." And in our classroom with their textbooks, we now find teacher who are themselves becoming redundant in 2011.

If the teacher is relational, and can speak on his or her own as a poet, then there is little need for the educational redundancies that even our language currently reminds us of. If the teacher is relational, then the classroom ceases to be a room that is the same as any other room of equivalent grade or subject matter. The classroom ceases to be a step on an assembly line. Instead, each classroom becomes itself a school—a school where unique relations are fostered by particular teachers. And if the teacher is a poet, then what is commonly known as a "textbook" becomes rather the content and context for poetry. Whatever subject matter there is to be learned becomes a new sort of subject—a subject for artistic rendition. A subject waiting to be interpreted by the student, not understood through some clarity of speech. Thus in 2011 and beyond, education might be informed by relation, enacted through poetry.

References

Bingham, C. (2002). A dangerous benefit: dialogue, discourse, and Michel Foucault's critique of repre-
    sentation. *Interchange, 33*(4), 351–369.
Bingham, C. (2008). *Authority is relational: Rethinking educational empowerment*. New York: State
    University of New York Press.
Bingham, C., & Biesta, G. (2010). *Jacques Rancière: Education, Truth, Emancipation*. New York:
    Continuum.
Bingham, C., & Sidorkin, A. (2004). *No education without relation*. New York: Peter Lang.
Khan Academy (2011a). http://www.khanacademy.org/about. Last Accessed 14 Apr 2011.
Khan Academy (2011b). http://www.khanacademy.org/#browse. Last Accessed 14 Apr 2011.
Williams, W.C. (1923). http://www.poets.org/viewmedia.php/prmMID/15537. Last Accessed 10 Apr 2011.

On the Essence of Education

Alexander M. Sidorkin

Published online: 5 June 2011
© Springer Science+Business Media B.V. 2011

Abstract   Educational reforms in developed countries are not successful, because we do not have a clear understanding of what is education. The essence of education is the limits of its improvement. Education is understood as the artificial extension of human ability to learn, as the product of learner's own efforts, and finally, as a series of historic forms of labor arrangements.

Keywords   Definition of education · Essence of education

The Pragmatic Essentialism

This is a contribution to the project of redefining the educational theory as a discipline, not merely as a field for application of other disciplines (Biesta 2012). If educational theory is a discipline, it should provide a unique lens to view the entire social world. Educational theory would then not only contemplate the world of schooling, or even the expanded world of educational experiences outside of schools. It would also offer an insight on the educational aspects of the economy, of politics, of communication, of culture, etc. Zooming out away from schooling allows zooming in on education.

Why is it important?—Because the world of mass schooling seems to be nearing a crossroads and we lack sufficient theoretical understanding to see where it can and cannot go next. Focusing on contemporary schools too narrowly limits our understanding of what education is and therefore what it can be. Identifying education with one of its historical manifestations creates a blind spot which makes radical rethinking of education difficult. We are bound too much to the tropes of classrooms, schools, students, and teachers to imagine how education can be otherwise. The education conceived as a field is incapable of providing answers, while the educational theory as a discipline may have a chance.

The need for essentialist thinking arises at the point where arbitrary definitions no longer work because of the overwhelming evidence of objectively existing limits which we do not

A. M. Sidorkin (✉)
Rhode Island College, Providence, RI, USA
e-mail: asidorkin@ric.edu

comprehend. A baby comprehends the essence of a stone when she tries to eat it, and cannot. Making noise with it, in contrast, works. Billions of babies come to similar conclusions about the nature of stone, and this background knowledge makes language and cooperation possible. Thus the essence of a phenomenon is tested through the collective human practice, and is revealed when such practice succeeds or fails. Essence is what we can and cannot do with any given kind of things. Let us call this approach the pragmatic essentialism.

Learning and Education

Education owes its existence to death. Another species that is immortal or nearly immortal would have a very slow or null rate of reproduction. Each individual would have plenty of time to learn everything slowly, and plenty of time to use the knowledge. Gods and immortals won't need education, because there is no rush to mature, and there are plenty of teachers. Such a species would no doubt outpace us in scientific and technological progress. They do not need set aside the tremendous resources dedicated to constant re-learning of everything, from alphabet to algorithms, every 70–90 years. We, however, live relatively short lives; too short for complex technological societies. The time spent on learning grows, while productive lives shorten. The trend can be compensated by growing productivity for only so long, because much of productivity depends on learning how to work and how to deal with machines that work for us. We have to learn fast, and as soon as we get good at anything, it is time to check out. One reason we abhor death is that is seems to be a tremendous waste of the most precious commodity: our own memory and skills. To cheat death, we keep inventing new and new forms of learning.

0. Learning 0.0, pre-learning, according to Darwin, is evolution itself. Each new generation "learns" something new, when the fittest survive. However, true learning begins when a single organism rather than a species can adapt.
1. Learning 1.0 according to B.F. Skinner; we share it with animals. It is simply learning from one's own individual experience. An important correction, which we can call Learning 1.5 have been made by Albert Bandura, and includes observational learning, also shared by most animals.
2. Learning 2.0 according to Vygotsky. Working together with a more advanced person seems to trigger faster learning about both the physical world and the social world. We learn ways invented by others, but not just through observation as in 1.5. This is where for the first time, teaching emerges. When people cooperate, the leader becomes a teacher.
3. Leaning 3.0 is schooling, which makes teaching and learning a matter of division of labor. To free up most adults from teaching, one teacher is put in charge of many students. It makes teaching cheaper, although not without a cost; let us call it the differentiation dilemma. Teachers need to accommodate individual pace and challenges unique to each student, which is hard to do for a group of students. Shared space requires common activities. Therefore children waste countless hours waiting for other children to learn what they already know, or because the material goes over their heads.

We should distinguish between Learning 3.1, schooling for the elites, and Learning 3.2, the mass schooling. The latter is a very different social institution, no longer based on the power to exclude, and therefore constantly troubled by low levels of learner motivation. This is where we are in the industrialized world, moving from 3.1 to 3.2. While at times it thinks as a very important transition, central to the essence of education, it should be viewed as just one small change, peculiar to our historical circumstances.

4. Learning 4.0 is only emerging. It promises to solve the differentiation dilemma brought with the help of information technology. The crude prototypes of self-training artificial intelligence can be found in Google, Face Book, Netflix, and Pandora algorithms. They may revolutionize learning within our lifetime, by learning from every student where she is, what works for her to learn better, and where she needs to go next. Teachers will concentrate on designing unique learning strategies for unique learning problems, and be freed from creating tasks for every student.
5. Learning 5.0 will defeat death itself. We will learn to extend our productive lives (and accordingly slow down our rate of reproduction). And/or, we will learn to download semantic memory more efficiently into our children's' minds.

Somewhere between 3.1 and 3.2, we exhausted the natural endowment of curiosity evolution allocated to our species. We had to invent ways of artificially extending our capacity and interest in learning. As species, we acquired too much knowledge to be transmitted in the natural way, and developed the need for artificial enhancements. The brief history of learning illustrates the relentless drive to learn more, more quickly, and more efficiently. Education is not identical to learning, as Biesta (2011) pointed out. It is a set of methods to make learning more efficient, faster, and more focused than it is would have occurred naturally. Education is learning that is enhanced, organized, and structured. Education to learning is what writing is to speech, vehicle is to walking, farming to gathering and husbandry to hunting. A clear understanding of this will prevent educators from continuously being enamored with the effortless ways in which little children learn. The illusion prevents them from seeing that education is, in essence, a response to the shortage of natural learning driven by the child's interest.

Learning as Doing

Education has always been examined and described by teachers. Learners did not have much of a say about it, because they are younger, less experienced, and less eloquent than teachers. By the time they are able to articulate better, they tend to switch camps and become teachers. That is why education has acquired the epistemological bias favoring teachers' point of view. It is often thought about in terms of teacher-student relationship; something that happens between the two. While the figure of a teacher is important in the contemporary modes of education, it is not necessary for educational to occur. Once a hunter starts practicing his archery on a target, he creates the elemental act of education. The transition from shooting at animals to target shooting is the move from simple learning to education. It requires a fundamental shift: the hunter must realize there is something within him—the skill of archery—that can be created separately and purposely. Education can also be described as purposeful making of internal tools—as opposed to the making of external tools. The ability to shoot arrows has to be manufactured in the sense very similar to manufacturing the bow and arrows.

A human being can do something for two distinct purposes: to transform the world and to transform herself. I will use Marx's and Engels description (1847):

> Bisher haben wir hauptsächlich nur die eine Seite der menschlichen Tätigkeit, die Bearbeitung der Natur durch die Menschen betrachtet. Die andre Seite, die Bearbeitung der Menschen durch die Menschen...

Before we have considered mainly only one side of human *Tätigkeit*, the processing of nature by the human intent. The other side, the processing of humans by other humans... (my translation)

Tätigkeit is normally translated as activity or occupation; it literally means *doingness*. "Occupation" sounds OK if used the way Dewey used it: "By occupation is not meant any kind of "busy work" or exercises that may be given to a child in order to keep him out of mischief or idleness when seated at his desk. By occupation I mean a mode of activity on the part of the child which reproduces, or runs parallel to, some form of work carried on in social life (1915, 131)." *Tätigkeit* is the kind of activity that transforms or creates something. But it is definitely not "activity," not *Aktivität*. The Russian equivalent *Деятельность* as used by Vygotsky and Leontiev is also very different from more generic *активность*. The latter is simply an opposite of being passive, the non-restful state of a living organism. The former has an object and a purpose.

Any *Tätigkeit* has the two sides to it; let us call them the object-transforming aspect (OTA) and the subject-transforming aspect (STA). For example, baking turns a lump of dough into a loaf of bread—this is the OTA. But the baker also learns something new, even infinitely small, with every loaf he bakes. Learning is everywhere, in every human *Tätigkeit,* and it constitutes the subject-transforming side of it. All subjects transform themselves in the act of doing. When the baker is a novice and the loaf turns into a pile of coals, the learning aspect of his activity stands out, becomes immediately visible. When he is baking his millionth loaf, the STA recedes into background and becomes infinitely thin, while the OTA becomes pronounced and dominating. But both aspects are always there. The hunter practicing his art of archery has very little chance to obtain food from shooting arrows at targets. The STA of this activity is infinitely more important than OTA. Education is practicing something – shooting arrows, baking, reading, writing, and thinking, researching, voting, and acting; anything done for practice.

Education is *Tätigkeit* where the subject-transforming aspect dominates the object-transforming. Sometimes this distinction is completely obvious, when the product of *Tätigkeit* is very much useless, and serves no other purpose than to be used for practice and be discarded. An intern working for a company produces a proposal that is much more likely to end up in the waste basket than those produced by regular workers, but it may actually be used to generate value. The distinction between education and production here is more probabilistic than deterministic.

The point of all this is that the heart of education is the learner's own work. It is what the learner is doing, and how she is doing it that makes certain kinds of *Tätigkeit* educational. Education is not what a teacher does to a student; it is what a student does to the world and through doing it, to herself. Teachers are managers and collaborators in this self-transforming work; they lead and help organize this work, but they are incapable of actually producing the change within the learner. You can lead a horse to water, but you can't make it drink; this is a description of the essential limits of education. It cannot be done for someone else. Learners produce the change within themselves by transforming something else.

Education as a Labor Arrangement

This means that education, at its core, is a specific labor arrangement. Since the natural capacity for learning is not sufficient to carry education, humans have devised a variety of ways to organize and incentivize the educational *Tätigkeit*. In other words, for a society to educate its next generation is to compel student to work on learning.

The two premises with which I begin are: (1) education is the artificial enhancement of learning, and (2) education is mainly the result of the learner's own purposeful *Tätigkeit*. If one accepts these, one should also agree that education requires a systematic application of learners' own effort not otherwise motivated by profit, pleasure or interest. That constituted labor of learners as an essential element of the entire educational enterprise.

History knows many labor arrangements used in education. The most common is the use of traditional expectations and of the power of familial relations. This ancient arrangement is still in place in many societies, where the authority of the family, clan, and community is directly transferred to the school. The combination of the patriarchal structure with modern economics is behind such educational "miracles."

> To put it simply, it is still possible to teach in the traditional way in Finland because teachers believe in their traditional role and pupils accept their traditional position. [T]he model pupil depicted in the strongly future-oriented PISA 2000 study seems to lean largely on the past, or at least the passing world, on the agrarian and pre-industrialized society, on the ethos of obedience and subjection that may be at its strongest in Finland among late modern European societies (Simola 2005).

Another form of labor arrangement is the use of selectivity. If a school is allowed to expel most or significant part of its students, it possesses a powerful enforcement mechanism. Schooling brings significant material benefits and cultural capital, distributed very unequally. This compels privileged students to keep working on learning, with a few exceptions of those truly opposed or allergic to schooling.

Yet another form of the educational labor arrangement is the state coercion. Authoritarian and totalitarian countries use it for all forms of labor, not just for learning. It is based on brutal force in combination with surveillance. The educational labor produced as a result of it, is not very productive but it creates the appearance of order. It would be fair to notice that democratic countries also use the administrative coercion method to keep children in schools. The compulsory education laws evolved as a reaction to limiting industrial child labor, but since have turned into an instrument of enforcement for another form of child labor, the educational labor of students in mass schools. Democracies are not necessarily democratic in their school policies; the societies that cherish individual rights may not afford granting the same rights to their youth.

The list would be incomplete without mentioning the ideology of Enlightenment. The idea is that a human being is incomplete without education, and that the pursuit of education is disinterested and noble. Although quite old, this method of labor enforcement is very much alive and active. Keeping the education discourse separate from economics is designed to create an additional incentive for children to work at the educational factories for free for many years. The discourse of Enlightenment is an actual means of production (Sidorkin 2011). Children convinced that education is a good thing produce actual economic value, for having an educated workforce and citizenry is an enormous public benefit. This arrangement has its limits, too. The over-production of discourse creates inflation. More and more students distrust the discourse, and create alternative cynical discourses. Without the backing of the state or the traditional family, the discourse of Enlightenment is a weakening force.

And one more mode of the educational labor arrangement is worth mentioning. It is based on an exchange: students contribute their educational labor, while progressive schools compensate them with entertainment, the sense of belonging and identity, and the life of the community (Sidorkin 1999). As all other methods above, it has serious limitations: students may find all of the good offered at a progressive school elsewhere: in mass media, neighborhoods, and other communities.

There are probably many more arrangements for educational labor. They all may be used in various combinations, complementing each other. This overview is only meant to be an example of labor analysis. It is also interesting to see what is not on the list. The largest proportion of all human labor on the planet is produced through capitalist labor markets. There are only small areas of volunteerism, domestic work of women, conscript armies, forced labor of prisoners, and remaining pockets of slavery and bound labor. All of them combined are not significant with respect to the total global labor output produced by paying people to work. The labor of students is an enormous exception: a form of non-free labor outside of monetary relations. Trying to pay children to learn is the next logical step in development of schooling.

It is also important to note that there is a fundamental limit to how much labor can be extracted from a human being, with or without force, with or without pay. It presents a limit for development of our civilization that it is worth considering. Some believe that the capacity for learning is unlimited, and that we can compel all of our children to work very diligently for as many years as we think appropriate. This is an unrealistic, utopian expectation steaming from misunderstanding of the essence of education.

Educational Theory as a Discipline

Educational theory can be construed as a discipline because of the ubiquity of the subject-transforming aspect in all kinds of *Tätigkeit*. Literally every organization, community, every enterprise can be analyzed from the point of view of the extent and the nature of learning that is happening in it. Organizations that are excellent on the object-transforming (OTA) side, may be quite light on the STA productivity, and vice versa. The task o educational theory is then to understand the relationships between the STA and OTA, which include assessing how various ratios between the two affect productivity and worker motivation. An educational consultant may bring a unique perspective to business: "Your quality controls are too rigid to allow for meaningful learning. You should allow for a small percentage of your output to be dedicated to learning, and therefore not to be intended for sale. You rely too much on work force that is already educated, which reduces the learning capacity of your organization. This is why your company cannot innovate anymore."

It is not clear to me that education should be so heavily concentrated in schools and so thinly represented in other organizations. Schooling itself is the product of the division of labor. The STA-rich forms of labor were put in one social institution, while OTA-rich activities remained in the main economy. But the may have gone too far. Humans evolved to value purposeful work with useful results. Schools are an aberration in this scheme of things. Schools are so ineffective because products of student work have no purpose other than to boost the skills and capacities of their producers. It is very difficult to convince children to do the work, results of which are discarded.

With this analytical lens, we should be able to say more about our own backyard, the schools. Can they increase their OTA to improve learning motivation? Almost nothing produced in schools is being consumed, or enters the market. Literally, every essay, every poem, every mathematical calculation students produce goes to the wastebasket. The great insight of Progressive Education was, in a way, to increase object-transforming aspect, making children's "occupations" look more like adult productive *Tätigkeit*. The mistake was to believe that all learning can happen through the OT-rich kinds of *Tätigkeit*. This is impossible for a variety of reasons, however it is very reasonable to learn the natural limits of such a plan, and to design better mixes of OT-rich and ST-rich areas of *Tätigkeit*.

Educational theory should understand how education is distributed throughout the society, and how it can be distributed better. How much teaching is really necessary, and how much of it is superfluous? Where do teachers act as teachers, and where do they simply enforce the compulsory education laws? Would it be actually less expensive to pay students to learn and have fewer, more specialized teachers aided by artificial intelligence? Those are the kinds of questions the true educational theory will consider.

References

Biesta, G. J. J. (2011). Philosophy of education for the public good: Five challenges and an agenda. *Educational Philosophy and Theory* (in press).

Biesta, G. J. J. (2012). On the idea of educational theory. In B. Irby, G. Brown, & R. Lara-Alecia (Eds.), *Handbook of educational theory*, Charlotte, NC: Information Age Publishing, Inc.

Dewey, J. (1915). *The school and society* (Revised ed.). Chicago: University of Chicago Press.

Marx, K., & Engels, F. *Die deutsche Ideologie*, orig 1846, http://www.mlwerke.de/me/me03/me03_anm.htm#M1.

Sidorkin, A. M. (1999). *Beyond discourse: Education, the self and dialogue*. Buffalo, NY: SUNY Press.

Sidorkin, A. M. (2011). Mad hatters, jackbooted managers, and the massification of higher education. *Educational Theory* (in press).

Simola, H. (2005). The Finnish miracle of PISA: Historical and sociological remarks on teaching and teacher education. *Comparative Education, 41*(4), 455–470.

Experimentum Scholae: The World Once More … But Not (Yet) Finished

Jan Masschelein

Published online: 9 June 2011
© Springer Science+Business Media B.V. 2011

Abstract   Inspired by Hannah Arendt, this contribution offers an exercise of thought as an attempt to distil anew the original spirit of what education means. It tries to articulate the event or happening that the word names, the experiences in which this happening manifests itself and the (material) forms that constitute it or make it find/take (its) place. Starting from the meaning of scholè as 'free time' or 'undestined and unfinished time' it further explores scholè as the time of attention which is the time of the regard for the world, of being present to it (or being in its presence), attending it, a time of delivery to the experience of the world, of exposure and effacing social subjectivities and orientations, a time filled with encounters. Education, then, relates to forms of profanation, suspension and attention and can be articulated as the art (the doing) and technology that makes scholè happen.

Keywords   Education · Experimentum scholae · Free time · Suspension · Profanation · Attention · World

> σχολή *(Greek: scholè): free time, rest, delay,*
> *study, discussion, lecture, school, school building*

At the end of her essay "What is Authority?" Hannah Arendt states that we are "confronted anew, without the religious trust in a sacred beginning and without the protection of traditional and therefore self-evident standards of behavior, by the elementary problems of human living together" (Arendt 1968a, p. 141). To take up this confrontation means to ask and investigate how to make sense again of such words as 'freedom' or 'authority', how to conceive of 'education', 'culture', etc. These are the "exercises of thought" that she

---

This essay could not have been written without Maarten Simons, who is to be seen in a true way and in the full sense as co-author.

J. Masschelein (✉)
Laboratory for Education and Society, Faculty of Psychology and Educational Sciences,
University Leuven, Vesaliusstraat 2, 3000 Leuven, Belgium
e-mail: jan.masschelein@ped.kuleuven.be

proposes in *Between Past and Future* starting from an acknowledgment that, in the strong sense, the meaning of these words has "evaporated", leaving behind "empty shells". The challenge they present is "to distil from them anew their original spirit" (Arendt 1968b, p. 15). Distilling the original spirit is neither to perform a historical reconstruction or genealogy, nor to engage in essentialist analysis in order to define a (suprahistorical) essence. It rather consists of attempts to relate these words to the experiences and mate- rialities connected to the inventions or events that they name and to our actual experiences. These exercises do not contain prescriptions on what to think or which truths to hold, they "do not attempt to design some sort of utopian future" (ibid. 14) or to provide definite solutions. The exercises of thought are to a large extent "experiments", attempts to clarify some issues and to "gain some assurance in confronting specific questions." Their literary form is that of the essay and the work that of an experimenter (ibid. 15). Let us, in this vein and with reference to a situation in which education seems to be conflated with facilitating (individual) learning processes and schools are being transforming from public institutions into privatized learning environments, risk such an exercise of thought as an attempt to distil anew the original spirit of what education means. This attempt is neither to define or clarify a concept, nor to project an idea, to purely describe a phenomenon, or to recall or explain (historical or empirical) facts. But it is trying to articulate the event or happening that the word names, the experiences in which this happening manifests itself and the (material) forms that constitute it or make it find/take (its) *place.*

In many languages the notion of 'school' (escuela, école, escuola, skola, Schule, etc.) derives from the Greek scholè ($\sigma \chi o \lambda \acute{\eta}$) which means first of all 'free time', but also: rest, delay, study, discussion, lecture, school building. All of these meanings are important and strongly related to each other and all of them would deserve a substantial elaboration, but let us take it, to begin with, in the sense of 'free time'. Free time is neither leisure time, nor the time of learning, development or growth, but the time of study, thought and exercise. We could call it also the time of the gap between what is possible and what is actual, or between past and future to use the words of Arendt. From this, we can take a straight- forward and preliminary articulation: Education is about *making* free or public time *happen*, to have the gap finding/taking (its) place. Or in other terms: it is about making 'school' in the sense of *scholè.* In this line, we can also state that the educator—e.g. the teacher as not only teaching but educating—is the one who leads to the school/scholè (which was the Greek meaning of the paedagogus—$\pi \alpha \iota \delta \alpha \gamma \omega \gamma \acute{o} \varsigma$) and/or contributes to its happening: the architect of scholè, i.e. the one who un-finishes, who undoes the appro- priation and destination of time. An educator (e.g. the teacher as educator) acts not only upon the opinion of equality of intelligence (as Jacques Rancière implies), which suspends the positions that are assigned in an unequal social, institutional order (which Rancière calls the police order), but she acts upon the opinion of time: there is free time and we have free time, that is, it is always possible to suspend defined or destined time. The psychol- ogist, the therapist, the pastor, the facilitator of learning assume no free time. Their time is destined or has a predefined sense or aim: the time of development or growth, the time of learning something, the time of salvation or progress, the time of optimisation and mobilisation, the time of reform and innovation, of investment and production (e.g. of learning outcomes). Scholè, however, is the time without destination and without aim or end.

School/scholè, then, is not to be conflated with the institution and, thus, can happen also outside it. In fact the school as institution could be regarded in many respects as a way to appropriate the school/scholè, to destine it. More generally we could read the history of the school as system/institution/organisation (and probably also the history of the philosophy of education that supported it) maybe to a rather large extent as a history of appropriation or taming of 'free time'.

Of course, one could say in a certain way that study, exercise or thought are the ends of scholè. But what we mean is that what appears, happens or is done within scholè is not determinated by a defined result, outcome or product. In this sense it is time which is freed from a defined end and therefore from the usual economy of time. The *Oxford Dictionary of English* traces the original sense of 'destination' and 'to destine' back to the Latin destinare: 'the action of intending someone or something for a purpose or end'. Free time as un-destined time is time where the act of appropriating or intending for a purpose or end is delayed or suspended. It therefore is also the time of rest (of being inoperative or not taking the regular effect) but also the time which rests or remains when purpose or end is delayed.

Free time as the time of study, thought and exercise is time which is separated from productive life, it is time where labour or work as economic activities are put at a distance. It is time of knowledge/matter for the sake of knowledge/matter (related to study), of capability for the sake of capability (connected to exercising) and of the voice/touch of an event in excess of the subject and its projects (which is at stake in thought). A typical feature of this separateness, then, is *suspension*. Economic, social, cultural, religious or political appropriations are suspended, as are the forces of the past and the future and the tasks and roles connected to specific places in the social order. To suspend means not to destroy or ignore, but to '*temporally* prevent from being in force or effect'. Education as a *form* of suspension is not destroying or denying anything, e.g. the past or the institutions, but is disorientating the institutions, interrupting the past. The necessities and obligations of professions, the imperatives of knowledge, the demands of society, the burden of the family, the projects for the future; everything is there or can be there, but in a condition of floating (see also: Barthes 1984).

Suspension here could be regarded more generally as an event of de-familiarisation, de-socialisation, de-appropriation or de-privatization; it sets something free. The term 'free', however, not only has the negative meaning of suspension (free from), but also a positive meaning, that is, free to. Drawing upon the terminology of Agamben, we can introduce the term *profanation* to describe this kind of freedom. According to Agamben "[p]ure, pro-fane, freed from sacred names is that thing that is being replaced in view of the common use by people" (Agamben 2005, p. 96). A condition of profane time is not a place of emptiness, therefore, but a condition in which things (practices, words) are disconnected from their regular use (in the family and in society) and hence it refers to a condition in which something of the world is open for common use. In that sense these things (practices, words) remain without end: means without an end, or un-finished.

The form of *suspension* and *profanation* is what makes scholè a public time; it is a time where words are not part (no longer, not yet) of a shared language, where things are not (no longer, not yet) a property and to be used according to familiar guidelines, where acts and movements are not (no longer, not yet) habits of a culture, where thinking is not (no longer, not yet) a system of thought. Things are 'put on the table', transforming them into common things, things that are at everyone's disposal for free use. What has been suspended is their 'economy', the reasons and objectives that define them during work or social, regular time. Things are thus disconnected from the established or sacred usages of the older generation in society but not yet appropriated by students or pupils as representatives of the new generation. The profane school/scholé functions as a kind of common place where nothing is shared but everything can be shared.

Comenius conceived of (school-)education as presenting the *world once more*, but according to him this 'once more' means to re-present the confusing, overwhelming world in an orderly, destined, defined way. School matter, then, refers to an oriented world (oriented beyond the confusion). However, in line with our reading of scholé, this orientation implies the taming of scholé. We would rather say, that the presentation of the world once more, without orientation or destination, turns something into school matter. That is the basis for what could be called the conservative aspect of education. This is not to be understood in the political sense to maintain the status quo, since it is precisely about offering or presenting the world once more without trying to define how it should be continued or used, i.e. to offer it un-destined, to set it free. That is why Arendt writes: "Our hope always hangs on the new which every generation brings; but precisely because we can base our hope only on this, we destroy everything if we so try to control the new that we, the old, can dictate how it will look" (Arendt 1968c, p. 189). That education is conservative means that it conserves things (words, practices) as unfinished things, i.e. things not directly related to an end, means without end so that students or pupils can begin anew *with* these things, *with* the world. They can now get meaning again, or get a new meaning.

Scholè is not simply a time of passage (*from* past *to* future), project-time or initiation-time. It is the time of attention which is the time of the regard for the world, of being present to it (or being in its presence), attending it, a time of delivery to the experience of the world, of exposure and effacing social subjectivities and orientations, a time filled with encounters.
    Michel Serres points our attention to the swimmer in the middle of a very large stream: "all security has vanished: there he abandons all reference points... The real passage occurs in the middle. Whatever direction determined by the swim, the ground lies dozens or hundreds of yards below the belly or miles behind and ahead. The voyager is alone. One must cross in order to know solitude, which is signaled by the disappearance of all reference points." (Serres 1997, p. 5). Taking this swimmer who traverses the stream it could look like the swimmer simply goes from one land to another (from the land of ignorance to that of knowledge for example), as if the medium would be simply a point without dimension (as when we jump). Of course, he 'arrives' in a second world, but more importantly, the swimmer did not only change river banks, but has known the trait that binds them and that is in fact a 'place' that integrates all directions, a 'milieu' that has no orientation itself, or, the other way round, opens to all directions and orientations. And we could add: human beings have no natural habitat, no proper place/milieu, no natural destination, which is the same as saying that they can experience scholè, and have to be educated (an animal that goes to school).

Profanation, suspension and attention are ways to communize and disclose world, and place students time and again in a position to begin (*with* the words, things): they offer the experience of being able, of potentiality in front of a thing in common. The words to 'communize' and 'communization' exist in English, but are seldomly used. They have their origin in communist theory where they refer to the process of abolishing ownership of the means of production and therefore resonate to the de-appropriation which we want to emphasize here, however in a somewhat different way. Communization is first of all—and perhaps only—an educational term, not a political one. As education presents the world once more, unfinished, it turns the world into a common thing, and puts students as equals in the position to begin. This is, if one would like, the political dimension of scholé. It needs no political doctrine and guidance—communist or not—to become political. The time and space of scholé has an end in itself or, which comes to the same, is a pure means, a medium.

Scholè can have different other names: the 'gap between past and future' (Arendt), a 'buble in time' (Pennac), a 'refugium' (Horkheimer), an 'asylum' (Deligny), a 'suspended garden' (Barthes). In all these cases it is a time/space where something can be and can become present and where we are in its presence (attentive and attending it, not only knowing but also concerned), so that it can touch us, and we can be in its company and can begin (to live) with it.

Where this something can start to signify, become a 'res' or 'thing' in the sense of Heidegger: referring to the old German word 'Ding' a thing is an affair, it is what assembles a world (Heidegger 1951). A thing is not an object of knowledge, but something that starts to (be of) interest, something that becomes part of our world, in the double sense of being part of it (and thus at once adding to it and further dividing it) and being of concern. The experience that is involved is the experience: 'it becomes interesting', which is at once an experience of de-appropriation and commonality. 'It' being, as Serres indicates, the third that repositions the first and the second person.

Education is not in the first place about the coming into presence of someone (a unique person), but of some thing as part of a common world. Some thing can communicate and become 'real' or realized (in the sense of being turned into 'res', into a 'thing'). In other words, scholè is where the world 'happens' (once more), is given again so that it becomes real and subjects are exposed to it, i.e. de-centered and de-subjectivated. De-centring and de-subjectivation are not the aim of scholè, but the consequence of something becoming 'real' (again). It is formative and transformative: a world takes place, 'things' appear, but in their appearing also the individual is transformed and co-appears and an interest in the sense of *inter-esse* can develop. That is why scholè is not so much about learning or about identity or subjectivity. The issue is not to know or learn who I am or who you or we are; the issue is to care for the self as being a care for what inter-ests. It is about the common world and what that world has to 'say' to me or us, how it 'interests' me or us. Scholè is the time of *being exposed together*.

And educators, than, don't re-present something, but through the way in which they deal with something (and thus communicate it)—their care or love for the world (their love for words, texts, things, practices), to refer once more to Arendt—they present some thing, they give some thing to see, to hear, and they let someone exist in the shadow of this thing. They give authority to some thing, bringing students or pupils in its neighbourhood so that it could become common or shared. The passionate teacher can make the matter speak, transform an object into a thing, that is a part of our world. Make that students come in touch and be touched, that is communicating and disclosing world.

Experimentum scholae: the experience of the happening, appearing and communizing of world.

But how to suspend time? How to disclose and communize world? This is not only to make the world known or to offer an immediate experience of a reality, but about the way in which a certain shaping or aesthetics obliges or incites us to take part in a sensory experience in which some thing is disclosed and communicated, such that the world divides and becomes shared, such that a purely detached relationship or dis-interested attitude becomes difficult to maintain and we become attentive. It is about an aesthetical arranging and dealing with matter (implying architecture, design, gestures, words, disciplines, composition, limitations, protocols) that places students or pupils in the silence of the beginning and offers the experience of potentiality in front of something.

Starting from the articulation of the event and experience of scholè, we could start to think of education as the art (the doing) and technology that (help) make it happen, i.e. spatializes, materializes and temporalizes this scholè. Education as practice, than, entails the tracing of *spaces*, the arranging and addressing of *matter* and the editing of *time* that make scholè (study, exercise, thought) happen. Starting from this first articulation, we could then try to reconsider and reinvestigate the rich pedagogic(al) and didactic tradition of practices and exercises in order to articulate them in terms of *pedagogic forms of suspension, profanation and attention*: the class, the lecture, the seminar, the workshop, the educational dialogue. (Foucault's lectures of the eighties would offer a brilliant start for such 'philosophy of education', including a morphology, figurology, technology and gesturology of education.) These forms would include particular architectures, particular pedagogic disciplines (intellectual and material technologies of mind and body, gestures) and pedagogical figures (persona characterized by a particular ethos, i.e. an attitude, disposition or 'stance' e.g. the figure of the teacher, professor, student), that constitute the happening of 'free time'.

Various ways exist in which 'free time' is neutralized or immunized in current discourses and educational technologies testifying of what one could call, by analogy with Rancière, a deep hatred of school. The banalization of school, which happens in the identification of the time of the school with the (natural) time of growth, maturation or development, with the (productive) time of learning or of political projects, masks/disguises the separation between 'useful, productive, economic time' and 'free time'. The banalization of the discussion and argumentation about a matter that takes place by reducing it to an exchange of private opinions and a debate on individual preferences, standpoints and perspectives masks the fact that in the school the (common) world is put into play (and not individual stakes or needs). The banalization of the teacher that takes place by identifying her with the professional, masks the possibility that she is an amateur, a lover of world, that can 'make' (free) time.

Moreover it is important to emphasize especially that free time (as is every time) is technologically mediated and edited, and that one of its basic mediums was apparently for a very long time alphabetic writing (which Ong called the technologisation of the word). Indeed, as Parry, Havelock, Ong, Illich, Sanders, Rotman and others have showed alphabetic recording of speech is the condition for the beginning of a 'pedagogical space' that implies the very coming into existence of words and of the difference between thought and speech. "Only the alphabet has the power to create 'language' and 'words', for the word does not emerge before it is written down" (Illich and Sanders 1988, p. 7) "Only then does true subject matter come into being; only then can the wisdom of a previous generation be transmitted in that generation's words, to be commented upon in distinct and new words by the teacher" (Ibid. 168). Without this alphabetical technologisation of the wor(l)d no 'education' and 'school'. Therefore, one of the crucial challenges seem to be whether and how scholè (as disclosure and communization), is to be made or sustained in a time of information and communication technologies, in a time of digital technologisation of the wor(l)d, in a time which is no longer that of modernization, progress or development, but of globalization and the instant.

Uncommon, perhaps, but it is necessary to end with us, the two authors of this essay. We came to experience that it is impossible to talk, to think and write alone about these things. Another, maybe the only name for that experience is friendship. Friendship is not about intimacy or privacy. It is a worldly experience; for friends the world becomes something of a concern, something to think about, something that provokes experimentation and writing. Is a philosophy of education, as far as it faces the world, possible without friendship? Clearly, it has never been, institutionally, more strongly required to indicate and claim one's own contribution, or at least to indicate an order of names. That reduces the time and space for friendship, it constitutes its banalization. Perhaps free time makes friends.

References

Agamben, G. (2005). *Profanations*. Paris: Payot.
Arendt, H. (1968a). What is Authorithy? In H. Arendt (Ed.), *Between past and future. Eight exercises in political thought* (pp. 91–141). New York: Penguin (1983).
Arendt, H. (1968b). The gap between past and future. In H. Arendt (Ed.), *Between past and future. Eight exercises in political thought* (pp. 3–15). New York: Penguin (1983).
Arendt, H. (1968c). The crisis in education. In H. Arendt (Ed.), *Between past and future. Eight excercises in political thought* (pp. 170–193). New York: Penguin (1983).
Barthes, R. (Ed.) (1984) Au séminaire. In *Essays critiques IV. Le Bruissement de la langue* (pp. 369–379). Paris: Seuil.
Heidegger, M. (1951) The thing. In M. Heidegger (Ed.) (1975): *Poetry, Language, Thought* (A. Hofstadter, Trans.). New York, London: Harper Colophon books.
Illich, Y., & Sanders, B. (1988). *ABC.The alphabetization of the popular mind*. London: Marion Boyars.
Serres, M. (1997). *The troubadour of knowledge*. Ann Arbor: The University of Michigan Press.

Coming Into the World, Uniqueness, and the Beautiful Risk of Education: An Interview with Gert Biesta by Philip Winter

PW Is there a theory of education in your work?

GB There probably is, although I have to say that this is more something that has emerged over the years than that it is something that I deliberately set out to develop. I have, of course, always been interested in theoretical and philosophical questions about education, but it was probably only when I started to work on my book *Beyond Learning* (Biesta 2006) that things came together and a theory of education emerged—and even then I was only able to articulate what this theory was about after I had finished the book.

PW Can you briefly describe what this theory is about and how it 'works'?

GB Sure. Conceptually it hangs on two notions: 'coming into the world' and uniqueness.' To understand why those notions are there and why they matter, I probably need to say a few things about the issues I was responding to in developing these ideas. The work on 'coming into the world' started in the late 1990s when I was invited to contribute to a conference on identity. When I started to explore that notion I realised a number of things. One was that I was actually not really interested in the question of *identity*—which for me is always the question of identification (identification by someone and/or identification with something) and therefore always articulates a third person perspective; identity is an explanatory concept, one could say—but much more in the question of *subjectivity*, that is the question of how we can be or become a subject of action and responsibility. For me that is the educational question, whereas identity is much more a sociological and psychological problematic.

By then I had already read enough of Foucault to understand that, unlike what many people still seem to think, the whole discussion about the death of the subject was not about the death of the very possibility of subjectivity—or 'subject-ness'—but rather was aimed at the idea that it is possible to speak the truth about the subject, that is, to claim to know what the subject is and to claim that it is possible to have such knowledge. One can of course

G. J. J. Biesta (ed.), *Making Sense of Education*, DOI: 10.1007/978-94-007-4017-4_16,   109
© Springer Science+Business Media Dordrecht 2012

treat this entirely as a philosophical matter, but I was interested in how the idea that it is possible to speak the truth about the human subject actually 'works,' that is, what it is doing and has been doing in a range of domains, including education and politics.

It was at that point that I realised that education—or as I now would say: *modern education*—tends to be based on a truth about the nature and destiny of the human being, a truth about what the child is and what the child must become, to put it in educational terms. Notions such as 'autonomy' and 'rationality' play an important role in modern educational thought and practice. While I'm all for autonomy and rationality, both notions are not without problems. Is it the case, for example, that we can ever be completely autonomous? What would that actually look like? And isn't it the case that the border between rationality and irrationality is historical and, in a sense, political rather than that it is simply 'there' or can be found deep down inside the human being? In addition to these more general and in a sense more philosophical questions, I was also concerned for those who may never be able to achieve autonomy or rationality. Are they beyond the scope of education? Are they outside of the sphere of politics? Are they beyond the scope of what it means to be human? The idea of speaking the truth about the human being was for me, therefore, not just as a philosophical question; for me it was first and foremost an educational, a political and an existential question. That is why I was less interested in trying to articulate what the subject *is*—which, when I pursued this theme in the writing of philosophers such as Heidegger, Levinas, Foucault and Derrida, was an impossibility anyway. I rather tried to find a language that could capture how the subject *exists*.

What I picked up from Jean Luc Nancy was the idea of 'coming into presence' which, for me, was a much more existential way to talk about the subject, one that referred to an *event* rather than an essence or identity, and one that expresses an interest in who comes into presence rather than that it tries to define what is to come, ought to come or is allowed to come into presence. The idea of 'coming into presence' thus turned traditional educational thinking on its head by not starting from what the child is to become, but by articulating an interest in that which announces itself as a new beginning, as newness, as natality, to use Arendt's term. What is crucial about the event of 'coming into presence' is that this is not something that can be done in isolation. To come into presence is always to come into the presence of *others*—which led me to an exploration of what one might call the relational dimensions of the event of subjectivity. Some of this was informed by my earlier work on pragmatism and the idea of intersubjectivity, but what I felt was missing from pragmatism was an awareness of what I would now call the deconstructive nature of 'coming into presence,' that is, the idea that the condition of possibility for anyone's 'coming into presence' is at the same time its conditions of impossibility. I drew some inspiration from the work of the Swiss architect Bernard Tschumi who, at the time, was arguing for a conception of architecture that included the way in which people make use of buildings and through this always interrupt the architectural programme. But the main inspiration came from Hannah Arendt and her notion of 'action.'

Arendt not only helped me to see that my coming into presence is always depends on how my beginnings are taken up by others. She also helped me to see that if we are committed to a world in which everyone's beginnings can come into presence, we have to live with the fact—which is actually not a fact but an articulation of what is means to exist politically (Biesta 2010a)—that the ways in which others take up my beginnings are radically beyond my control. The very condition that makes my 'coming into presence' possible—that is, the fact that others take up my beginnings—also disrupts the purity of my beginnings, so to speak, as others should have the freedom to take up my beginnings in their own ways. Arendt's intriguing phrase 'plurality is the condition of human action' still captures this very well, as it is only under the condition of plurality that *everyone's* beginnings can come into presence, and not just the beginnings of one single individual. It is because of this line of thinking that I shifted from the notion of 'coming into presence' to the notion of 'coming into the world,' The main reason for this was to highlight what I see as the inherently political nature of the event of subjectivity, that is, the fact that the event of subjectivity can only happen in a world of plurality and difference—a *polis* or public sphere, so we might say. Educationally all this means that the responsibility of the educator can never only be directed towards individuals—individual children—and their 'coming into presence' but also needs to be directed to the maintenance of a space in which, as Arendt puts it, 'freedom can appear.' It is, therefore, a double responsibility: for the child *and* for the world and, more specifically, for the 'worldly' quality of the world.

PW And what about uniqueness?

GB The idea of uniqueness is important because if we only were to have the idea of 'coming into the world,' we would have an account of how the event of subjectivity occurs—we would have a theory of subjectivity, to put it differently—but we would not have an argument for why the subjectivity of each single subject who comes into the world might matter. That is why the idea of 'coming into the world' needs to be complemented by a notion of 'uniqueness.' But there are two ways in which uniqueness can be articulated—one which brings us back to identity and questions about knowledge of the subject, and one which leads us to an existential argument. I my work I have articulated this as the distinction between 'uniqueness-as-difference' and 'uniqueness-as-irreplaceability' (Biesta 2010b)—and the inspiration for the latter approach comes from Emmanuel Levinas. Uniqueness as difference focuses on our characteristics, on what we *have*, and articulates how each of us is in some respect different from everyone else. Again we could say that this is a third person perspective, but what is more problematic here is that uniqueness-as-difference is based on an instrumental relationship with the other: we need others in order to articulate that we are different from them, but that's all that we need the other for. Uniqueness-as-irreplaceability, on the other hand, brings in a different question: not what *makes* me unique, but *when does it matter* that I am I? The brief answer to this question is that this matters when I am being addressed, when someone appeals to me, when someone calls me. Those are situations in which I am singled out by the other, so to speak. And in those situations—if the other is after *me*, not after me in my social role (which would be my identity)—we are irreplaceable; or to be more precise: we are irreplaceable in our responsibility for the other. Whether we take up this responsibility, whether we take responsibility for our responsibility, to use Zygmunt Bauman's phrase, is entirely up to us. There is no theory that can tell us that we should do this. Nor can the other command that I should take up my responsibility. This is entirely up to me. In this sense, therefore, the idea of uniqueness-as-irreplaceability not only articulates a first person perspective, but is also entirely existential. It claims nothing about what the subject *is*—just about situation we can find ourselves in, situations in which we are literally singled out and in which our uniqueness matters. I still find this quite a powerful way to engage with the event of subjectivity—and also a quite beautiful way, actually. I don't see it as a theory of subjectivity but have rather called it an 'ethics of subjectivity' (Biesta 2008)—as the question of subjectivity, of the event of subjectivity, is approached in ethical terms, rather than in epistemological or ontological ones, which is another way of saying that about the human subject there is nothing to know.

PW How does this relate to 'coming into the world'?

GB Well, in a sense it specifies how uniqueness can come into the world. But uniqueness is an event, not something the individual can possess or claim to possess (or claim to know for that matter). As an event it is therefore something that always is at stake, where there is always the question whether the event of subjectivity can be achieved—which is perhaps already a bit too active as a term.

PW What can educators do with these ideas?

GB Very little, actually—that is, if you take doing in the Aristotelian sense of *poiesis*, that is to think of doing as production. And there is of course a long tradition in which education is understood along those lines, that is, as a process that needs to produce something, that needs to have certain outcomes, as in the currently all too popular phrase of 'learning outcomes.' But we do not produce out students; we are there to teach them—just as we do not make our children; they are born to us. Subjectivity, therefore, is precisely *not* an outcome and even less a learning outcome; it is precisely *not* a thing that can be produced—which is why I like the idea of the *event* of subjectivity and of subjectivity-as-event so much. But it leads to a certain predicament for educators in that on the one hand I am arguing—and I am not alone in arguing this but am connecting to a long educational tradition—that the question of subjectivity should be a prime educational interest, whereas on the other hand I seem to be saying that there is nothing that educators can do.

My response to this predicament is to argue that while subjectivity cannot be *produced* through education—or for that matter politics—it is actually quite easy to *prevent* the event of subjectivity from occurring. If the event of subjectivity has to do with the ways in which I can be addressed by the other, by the otherness of the other, it is quite easy, both at the individual level and at the institutional level, to create situations in which the possibility for being addressed is edited out, where, as Jan Masschelein has put it, we become immunised for the call of the other, where we put up our fences, close our eyes and ears—and perhaps even our hearts—and eradicate the very risk of being interrupted by the other, the risk of being addressed by the other, of being put into question by the other, to use a Levinasian phrase. And that is perhaps the greatest problem with making education into a risk-free experience, into a zone where we can no longer be put into question, where we can no longer be addressed, where we can no longer be touched, where I am never at stake, so to speak. To make education 100% safe, to make it 100% risk-free thus means that education becomes fundamentally un-educational. That is why the risk of education—what I tend to call the *beautiful* risk of education—is so very important; but I am that it is not fashionable to argue that education ought to be risky.

PW Does that also lie behind your critique of certain tendencies in educational research? I'm thinking here, for example, of your critique of evidence-based education in your "Why what works won't work" essay (Biesta 2007).

GB Absolutely. The whole idea of evidence-based education is again based on the erad-ication of risk and a desire for total control over the educational process. There are a number of issues here. One has to do with the assumptions about educational processes and practices that inform the conception of research that is promoted here. The assumption is that education can be understood as a causal process—a process of production—and that the knowledge we need is about the causal connections between inputs and outcomes. I don't think that education is such a process—and I also don't think that education should be *understood* as such a process or, even worse, should be *modelled* as such a process. The latter point is important because I do think that it is, in principle, possible to model education as a causal process, that is, to make it into a process that operates in a causal way. This can be done by radically reducing the complexity of the educational process (Biesta 2010c). This requires that we control *all* the factors that potentially influence the connection between educational inputs and educational outcomes. This can be done, but it is a huge effort, which not only raises the question whether it's worth the effort—the Soviet Union wasn't able to sustain the total control of its citizens, and probably North-Korea will not be able to sustain it in the end—and also whether the effort is desirable, and when you take it to its extremes it's quite obvious that the effort is ultimately not desirable. But it is a slippery slope, and in a lot of countries education is rapidly moving in this direction and is becoming oppressive, not only for those at the receiving end—students—but perhaps even more so for those who have to work under such oppressive conditions, teachers, school leaders and administrators.

PW Is there a risk that you create a rather black and white picture, where it is either control or freedom, either causality or total openness?

GB That's a fair point, and it actually has to do with one of the things I realised after the publication of *Beyond Learning*, which is that while the question of subjectivity is a very important and, in a sense, both essential and fundamental dimension of education, it is not the be all and end all of education. That is why, in my book *Good education in an age of measurement* (Biesta 2010a), I argued that education, particularly school education, not only functions with regard to human subjectivity, but performs other functions as well. In the book I refer to those other functions as qualification—this is the domain of knowledge, skills and dispositions—and socialisation—which I defined as the way in which, through education, we become part of existing 'orders' (social orders, political orders, cultural orders, religious orders, professional orders, and so on). I think that it is important to be aware that education functions in these three domains. But I also see these three domains as three dimensions of educational purpose, that is, three dimensions in which educators can claim that education should function, should make an impact. Perhaps—but I still want to say this with great caution—questions about relationships between inputs and outcomes, questions about making education 'work,' have a place where it concerns the qualification and socialisation dimension of education. After all, if we want our students to learn complex skills—like flying a Boeing triple-7, performing brain surgery, but actually in the whole domain of skills, including car mechanics, plumbing, etcetera—we want to make sure that our students get it 'right' (which for me always also include the need for students to be able to make judgements about what it means to get it right, plus the ability to judge when getting it right is not what is needed in a particular situation). So we have to be mindful that education is not just about the question of the subject. But at the same time I would also say that if this dimension falls out—if it disappears from the scene, if it is no longer considered to be relevant, then we have ended up in an *un*educational space. The art of teaching, in my view, is precisely that of finding the right balance between the three dimensions, and this is an ongoing task, not something that can be pre-programmed or sorted out by research.

PW A final question then: what is the place of democracy in your theory of education?

GB While in what I have said so far I haven't used the word 'democracy' I hope that it is clear that there is a strong democratic 'sentiment' in the way in which I look at education. For me it goes back to the connection between subjectivity-as-event and the idea that the event of subjectivity is only possible under the condition of plurality. That, in a sense, is where the democratic ethos and the educational ethos come together and perhaps even coincide. That is why, for me, the democratic is at the very heart of the educational—it's not an add-on, but it is what is at stake if we see the event of subjectivity in the way in which I have tried to approach it.

PW Thank you very much.

References

Biesta, G. J. J. (2006). *Beyond learning. Democratic education for a human future.* Boulder, Co: Paradigm Publishers.

Biesta, G. J. J. (2007). Why 'what works' won't work. Evidence-based practice and the democratic deficit of educational research. *Educational Theory, 57*(1), 1–22.

Biesta, G. J. J. (2008). Pedagogy with empty hands: Levinas, education and the question of being human. In D. Egéa-Kuehne (Ed.), *Levinas and education: At the intersection of faith and reason* (pp. 198–210). London/New York: Routledge.

Biesta, G. J. J. (2010a). How to exist politically and learn from it: Hannah Arendt and the problem of democratic education. *Teachers College Record, 112*(2), 558–577.

Biesta, G. J. J. (2010b). *Good education in an age of measurement: Ethics, politics, democracy.* Boulder, Co: Paradigm Publishers.

Biesta, G. J. J. (2010c). Five theses on complexity reduction and its politics. In D. C. Osberg & G. J. J. Biesta (Eds.), *Complexity theory and the politics of education* (pp. 5–13). Rotterdam/Boston/Taipei: Sense Publishers.

Index

G. J. J. Biesta (ed.), *Making Sense of Education*, DOI: 10.1007/978-94-007-4017-4,
© Springer Science+Business Media Dordrecht 2012

Printed by Printforce, the Netherlands